LIVING BIBLICALLY

"I guarantee you will not be able to put this book down. Sisters Rosie and Rebekah write in a style crystal clear and magically engaging, all the while gleefully butchering sacred cultural cows and serving up a feast of rich, meaty delights for anyone, especially any Christian woman, who has found herself wresting with what it means to be a child of God in today's world. You're gonna love this book, even as its wit and brainy argumentation stretch you to new limits of genuine Christian faith, love, and piety."

—Rev. Matthew C. Harrison, President,
The Lutheran Church—Missouri Synod

☙❧

"One of the best 'hear and do' pieces I've read, out of hundreds. Rosie and Becky are freedom fighters and, in the sacred sense, burden bearers of women's issues! Lost your voice amidst the chaos of 21st-century womanhood? Find it here. Not to scream or demand, but to follow Christ into contentment, fulfillment and with gusto resist the pull of lesser gods. It is impossible to put it down!"

—Phyllis Wallace, Author, Speaker, Broadcaster

☙❧

"Adle and Curtis don't pull any punches in their dash to ride the countercultural wave of biblical truth about womanhood as Christ designed and redeemed her. With a healthy dose of sardonic wit, spiced with the right dash of caregiving reserve, their work is a breath of fresh air in a world of women caught up in the maelstrom of not being 'good enough' unless they try to be men."

—Rev. Jonathan Fisk, Pastor, Host of *Worldview Everlasting* and
Author of *Broken: 7 "Christian" Rules That Every Christian
Ought to Break as Often as Possible*

☙❧

"*LadyLike* strips away all flowery cross-stitch stereotypes while exposing the burlap of what it means to be a Christian woman in 21st-century society. Adle and Curtis hold nothing back as they take an uppercut at the lies of our modern era, simultaneously weaving in the delicate ribbons of mercy found in Christ's timeless truth. These essays are at once strong and sassy, while maintaining the graceful art of what it means to be a woman in Christ. They contain the healing balm of Christ and Him crucified that is vital for staying the course on the lonely road of being a Christian woman, Christian mother, and Christian wife in today's world—a balm so soothing that the reader is left wanting more."

—Meridith Fisk, Wife, Mother, and Homemaker

೮৩

"In this well-written book, Rose and Rebekah challenge women with clever, yet honest truths served up with a 'delicious gulp of Gospel.' Their striking insights and crisp language encourage us to see our lives in new ways. You will be blessed!"

—Renee Gibbs, Teacher, Speaker, Mentor

೮৩

REBEKAH CURTIS *and* ROSE ADLE

LADY
LIKE

LIVING

BIBLICALLY

CONCORDIA PUBLISHING HOUSE · SAINT LOUIS

Published 2015 by Concordia Publishing House
3558 S. Jefferson Ave., St. Louis, MO 63118-3968
1-800-325-3040 • www.cph.org

1 2 3 4 5 6 7 8 9 10   24 23 22 21 20 19 18 17 16 15

CONTENTS

FOREWORD

Our society loves open and honest dialogue. We want to discuss the hard issues and to be challenged intellectually. And we appreciate the maverick, the innovator, and the one who brings fresh ideas to the table. Or at least that's what we tell ourselves. This book is bound to test our claims. Quite frankly, I can't say I've read anything like it. *LadyLike* is, quite simply, stunning. What a title! I might describe it as radically retro, freshly old-fashioned, and powerfully submissive. In light and lovely prose, Rosie Adle and Rebekah Curtis, two playful and mischievous sisters, challenge us to rethink everything we thought we knew about men and women. Like a jolt of espresso, or a polar bear plunge, their writing enlivens the senses, helping us to see the world, as it were, for the first time. In a society where conversations about gender have too often become stale and predictable, Rosie and Rebekah reimagine what it means to be a Christian woman in our feminized secular society.

For example, Rosie and Rebekah compare life to a pie-eating contest. I know it sounds crazy, and it is, but in a good way. Feminism encourages women to take in everything that life has to offer, with the result that they feel both bloated and unsatisfied, overwhelmed and empty. "We trudge along, fork in, fork out. We're always looking for our Tums and wondering how we'll handle the giant pile of plates accumulating in our kitchen sink," they write. Can today's woman have it all? Should she even want to have it all? Whatever you might think, after reading this essay, you're bound to want another slice of what they have to offer.

Each chapter is just a couple of pages, rich and satisfying. You might want to read an essay before bed, and let their words roll around your brain as you fall off to sleep. Or maybe, like me, you'll devour the whole thing in a single sitting and then come back for more later. The topics are often provocative. Was Jesus a feminist? Was the Old Testament misogynistic? What about 50 *Shades of Grey*? And perhaps most intriguing, who's supposed to wash the dishes? Each essay is sure to spark conversations, even debates. You might be taken aback, even shocked, but you sure won't be bored. Rosie and Rebekah are a paradox, something our cultures tells us cannot exist. These women exude confidence but preach submission. They encourage the cultivation of the mind and yet treasure domesticity. They call us back to a time, as Archie Bunker used to sing, "when girls were girls and men were men." And they do so with good cheer. It's Christian girl power, a dose of empowerment, and a celebration of the feminine virtues rediscovered. In the spirit of the biblical Deborah, Rosie and Rebekah are warriors but also feminine to the core, and proudly so.

Some may compare this work to that of other contemporary Christian authors like Beth Moore or Joyce Meyer. But that would be a disservice. Rosie and Rebekah are at once more serious and much more fun, certainly more challenging and biblical to boot. Rosie and Rebekah love the Church, but they're not church mice. Turn the pages, and you'll hear them roar. They speak of what they call "women's work," and they do so unashamedly. They advocate for pastors who are men, real men of God. They analyze our culture, and do so with lively illustrations, all along sharing the common frustrations of today's woman. And to bring it all home, they take us on a tour of what the Bible has to say about men, women, and marriage, including side trips in which they explore what it means to be celibate, what it feels like to be barren, and how to struggle against temptation. If you come to this book with modernist assumptions, you may, at times, become infuriated. If you come expecting bland reassurance, you're sure to be jolted. You might, every once in a while, feel like your toes have been stepped on and ask, "Who do they think they are?" But you won't be bored, and if you let down your guard, you might find yourself smiling, even laughing alongside these women. They're funny and compassionate, and you get the feeling that they're on your side. These women clearly love being women, but they also know how difficult, strange, and even absurd life's journey can be. And they know the joy of the journey when Christ is by your side.

On a side note, when I was asked to look at *LadyLike*, Rosie told me, somewhat in jest, that I might be one of the only men who ever reads it. That would be a pity. While this work is clearly aimed at young, strong, smart, Christian women, any man would do himself a favor reading what these two women have to say. So buy a copy for your wife or girlfriend, mother or daughter, and when she's done reading it, borrow it from her. After all, Christian women deserve good Christian men. And when it comes to God's will, we'd all do well to surrender, I happily submit.

—Dr. Peter J. Scaer

INTRODUCTION

We wrote this book with women in mind—all kinds! Single or married, young or not young, this or that, we thought of you. Not every essay will speak immediately to every woman's own life. But we hope that all readers will find relevance and support particular to their circumstances somewhere in this book, and probably on several occasions. If it's not about you, it's about someone you love and would like to love better.

These essays aren't devotions or inspirations. If you're looking for instant insights in pretty fonts, we'll be happy to see you on Pinterest because we're girls too! But what we're offering here are thoughts aimed to ground our functions, identities, and lives in Christ our Lord as He reveals Himself to us in His Word.

He is the Author and Perfecter of our faith, after all. Let's fix our eyes on Him, right?

Adle and Curtis

Out of Order

There is an order to the world. You (whoever you are) are not at the top. Satan lied when he said that we could be more like God by doing something that God explicitly forbade. When Eve and Adam sank their teeth in, they became aware of good and evil, and that they were on the wrong side of that line. This placed them *farther* from God, not closer. Instead of joining God for a stroll in the cool of the day, they ran and hid.

Genesis 1 and 2 detail the order: God > man > woman > animals. This is described in the New Testament too. First Corinthians 11:3 explains, "I want you to understand that the head of every man is Christ, the head of a wife is her husband, and the head of Christ is God." This fuller description of the order is Father > Son > man > woman. Ephesians 5:23 speaks the same way: "For the husband is the head of the wife even as Christ is the head of the church, His body, and is Himself its Savior."

This is the good arrangement designed by God. Even the Trinity has an ordering. It does not mean that the Son is somehow less God than the Father is, nor is woman less human than man, but there is order. God is a God of order, not of confusion. Order is good. Patriarchy is the earthly arrangement God ordained. Adam is created first and given charge. Eve is to help him. They are to subdue and rule the earth.

Then, in Genesis 3, one of the creeping things of the earth comes to tempt the woman. Hey! Isn't she supposed to be above him? Why is she taking cues from him? Uh-oh. And hey! Where is Adam? He is *with* her (v. 6), but it is not reported that he says anything to deter her. In fact, he not only tolerates her disobedience, he joins her in it. Total overturn of the order! Now it stands serpent/Satan > woman > man. And none of them are paying attention to God. Disregarding the divinely established arrangement, Eve listens to the serpent instead of turning to Adam or God. Adam sits idly by while this goes on, and this causes *all* to fall (Romans 5:12).

This is terrible. It brings about death, infuses hardship in vocations, causes sin to spread to the progeny they would bear, and subjects the rest of creation to futility (Genesis 3:17; Romans 8:20).

Is everything wrecked, totally wrecked? Is everything permanently out of order? Thanks be to God, it isn't. Order is what God reemphasizes when He shows up on the scene. When He comes looking for His fallen creatures, He calls for Adam (Genesis 3:9). Eve may have been the one who spoke to the serpent and first ate the forbidden fruit, but Adam is responsible because he is the head.

He finds them (He's God! They're not! Who did we think would win the hide-and-seek game?) and it's time for punishment. Genesis 3:14–19 is often called "the curse," and it is true that God speaks of bad things to come. All told though, it is a rather good sermon containing *both* Law and Gospel. During that speech, God puts things back in order because that is His gracious nature.

For the serpent who exalted himself, on his belly he would go (v. 14). For the woman who listened to one of the creeping things of the earth, her seed would crush the serpent's head (v. 15). And even when she would desire to master her husband, the man would still rule over her (v. 16). For Adam, who listened to his wife and the serpent, he would still work and provide, but it would be through pain, toil, and sweat (vv. 17–19). There is indeed a curse involved, as man would return to the dust from which he was made, but this speech by God also tells of the coming defeat of the serpent/Satan, and it sets things back in order. Because of sin, the going would be tough, but there *would* still be going. Adam would still be the breadwinner, Eve would still be the mother and helper, and they could both look forward to the Seed promised by God.

How can this be, though? How can it be God's plan that we live this way? Isn't patriarchy the root of all evil and the reason we live in a sexist world filled with harassment, stereotypical expectations of women, and unequal pay for equal work?

A world where man is head of woman is a world where a sinner will be head of a sinner. That much is true. This is why we, along with the rest of creation, groan. The order won't ever be occupied perfectly by us sinners this side of the resurrection of the body and the life everlasting. Men won't be perfect heads and women won't be perfect helpers, and so often both reject the place in the order for which we were all created.

But is the system itself bad by design? Does it necessarily produce abuses, inequalities, and injustices? No. The order God set up is not inherently bad. It was part of His original creation, and it, along with all the rest, was good. Furthermore, it was not just descriptive of Adam and Eve. It is prescriptive for all of us for all of time. Ephesians 5 confirms this. For all eternity, Christ will remain the Head of His Bride, the Church.

There will always be authority. There will always be an order of creation. To live otherwise is to be out of order. When we see a sign with those words printed on it, we know the ideal outcome is repair and restoration. That is exactly what God has promised us (Acts 3:21). So we keep at it, with God's help! We women know our place, and we know it's a good one because it's the one the Lord lovingly and thoughtfully designed for us.

The Pie-Eating Contest

A little girl walked into a kitchen and saw a delicious pie on the table. (French silk, if I'm the one calling the shots, but that's not central to the story.) The little girl squealed with delight, "I want to eat it all!"

"You can't have it all," her mother replied. "It wouldn't be good for you."

End of discussion.

Many years later, another kitchen and another pie. This time, there's a different response.

It smells so good! It looks so good! The girl, now a grown woman, squeals, "I want to eat it all!" And everyone cheers. Yes to the pie! Yes to the eating of it all! Go you!

She starts in on the pie and life is sweet. After a few large slices, she's a little bit surprised that having it all is not as easy or as enjoyable as she had anticipated. She keeps slugging along. Pie, pie, pie, pie. She was the one who asked for this in the first place. She'd better get through it, and she'd better do it with a smile on her face and two thumbs-up. Those later slices don't taste nearly as good as the earlier ones. She keeps forcing them down though. Yum! Yum. Yum? Ugh.

By now, her stomach is positively churning, producing all manner of sounds and sensations. The gluttonous undertaking overwhelms her digestive system. Her body tries to process the sugar coursing through her system, but it isn't going too well. All that sweetness seemed energizing at first, but now there are threatening signs of a system-wide crash. The exertion of the task leaves even her teeth hurting. Thoughts of "Not worth it" and "Why?" flood her mind. This really isn't what she was counting on. While eating the whole pie is possible and permissible, it sure ain't pretty.

Women keep hearing that we can have it all. We can earn flashy degrees. We can have meaningful work in any field of interest. We can have a family. We can travel. We can write a book (wait, what?). We make it all hum without losing our figure or our sanity or our *joie de vivre*. We can have it all.

The entire pie is tempting. It almost feels wasteful *not* to eat it all. What about those other slices? What would become of them? Gone is the mother who said matter-of-factly, "You can't have it all. It wouldn't be good for you." New mom on the block has a pretty hefty investment in the eating.

"Think about it," she reasons. "What would become of those slices you don't eat? Go for it now while you're young and have a strong stomach. Otherwise, those untouched slices will get old and dry up, and they won't be any good when you finally have an appetite for them. And let's not forget that my friends and I worked hard to make this whole pie business possible for you in the first place, soooo . . ."

While it was once understood that eating a whole pie would be overwhelming, taxing, and generally ill-advised, now the pressure is on. "You can have it all" goes in one ear, and by the time it's done rattling around in our brain for a while, it sounds a lot more like "You'd better have it all," or "You'll be missing out if you don't," or "You'll look weak if you can't handle it."

Women are biting off a lot. And in the tremendous task of chewing, swallowing, and digesting, many are feeling the effects of the have-it-all lifestyle. We're tired a lot. We're sick a lot. We feel like we're actually missing out on some of life's sweetest moments by having it all. How can we savor and enjoy any one bite or any one slice while we're cramming it all down our throats so relentlessly?

But we look around and other ladies seem to be down-ing their pies just fine. They are climbing the ladder. They are busting through the legendary glass ceiling. They're do-ing these things while arriving everywhere on time, thawing quinoa-based freezer meals, and hitting the gym for their mandatory "me" time. Their husbands adore them, and their kids win every spelling bee. It seems like the system is working for them, which makes the rest of us feel all the more discouraged.

We trudge along, fork in, fork out. We're always looking for our Tums and wondering how we'll handle the giant pile of pie plates accumulating in our kitchen sink. "What's wrong with me? Why is this making me nauseous when the other gals are happily scarfing down the delicacies of this liberated life?" More pie. More pie. More pie.

My hunch? By the end of the pie-eating contest, even the winners feel a little sick.

Products of Our Time

Oh, the bad old days. They were so bad! The men sat on one side, the women sat on the other. Only men were allowed to vote. Women were supposed to get married, have kids, and do nothing but take care of them. Dads never changed diapers; husbands couldn't make their own breakfasts. Males were known to be intelligent and rational, while females were flighty and emotional. It's hard to believe anyone—or at least any woman—could ever have thought that way.

That is to say, *now* it's hard to believe people once thought that way. The world's way of thinking about men and women has had a complete overhaul in the last century. While not all women consider themselves feminists, they are living in a society much closer to the feminist vision than the society out of which that vision grew. Now a dad who doesn't do diapers is a colossal jerk, the franchise is available to any nonfelon with a pulse, and every profession and/or trade is so open to women that many women have no choice but to give most of their energy to working in one (flooding the workplace with workers wasn't a great plan for keeping wages high).

How foolish we would be to believe that our immersion in this society has not shaped the way we think. It is patronizing and disrespectful to imagine that women one hundred years ago were unable to reason as we are today simply because they saw the world differently than we do. Human intelligence being roughly equal, there must be some other explanation. "But they were products of their time," we protest. Indeed they were, but how can we be any less? We all live some*time*. "And they were uneducated!" we add in triumph. The level of literacy required on eighth-grade exams from the nineteenth century calls this argument into serious question. But let's accept the point: our educational system offers more years of education to more women than it did a century ago. On the other hand, how many of us arrived at our view on women holding public office because school forced us to be briefly familiar with terms like *asymptote*, *participle*, or *torque*, and to perform some related tricks? The academy is the world's stooge. The world was in full control of telling us what we should think of it when we happened to be passing through, and nobody said boo about the conflict of interests. So much for education.

This is how the Christian knows she must proceed with caution. This world is not our home (John 17:14), and for this we can be grateful. The world is where every act of human evil has been conceived, cultivated, and perfected. It is the opposite of the kingdom of God, the true home of every child of God. We should not be surprised, then, that the Church and the world look so different. One time in human history, the Church distinguished itself with its opposition to a status quo where might made right. Women are the group of people most obviously benefited by social mores that prioritize protection of the weak and peaceful resolution of conflicts. Christianity has always been the force behind the belief that women are human, and as such should not be robbed, roughed up, or raped by those with the strength to do so.

The Church is still being called upon to make this argument, although history now demands it from a different corner. Now it falls to the Church to insist that not all humans must be men. Only the Church is willing to acknowledge that the comparative physical weakness of women is a fact that demands deferential behaviors on the parts of both men and women (1 Peter 3). The Church is the only place where celibacy is honored equally in men and women (1 Corinthians 7), whereas the world smirks at the unmarried woman, who obviously has something wrong with her. The Church is the only place where a woman whose primary credential is motherhood is honored rather than derided because the Church sees motherhood as a divine blessing of intrinsic value (Psalm 128). Only Christianity applies its sexual ethos indiscriminately, never sighing "boys will be boys" as if a system ultimately based in the union of two parties could operate effectively with the two parties adhering to different ethics. It refuses to solve the problem of boys being boys with the specious conclusion that girls should also be boys.

What is the Church, and particularly her women, saying by insisting upon certain unenlightened practices? Not necessarily that the world was better when men didn't wash dishes, but also not that the world was worse. In the Piers Anthony science fiction novel *Fractal Mode*, a woman from another world is on a quest to change her world's orientation from male control to female (this is to be accomplished by a magic person flipping some kind of cosmic switch, bypassing the trouble we earthlings have had to endure). The other characters want to know how this will solve her world's problems. After giving it some thought, she realizes that the problems won't change. There will just be a different set of people causing them.

While Piers Anthony is at least as feminist as everyone born after 1930, as a high priest of culture, he stands here in the place of Caiaphas, prophesying the truth by virtue of his office. Feminism has not made women's lives better, easier, or safer. At best, it has made them differently difficult. Demanding that rape be a topic of incessant public conversation has not meant less rape when feminism simultaneously demanded sexual "freedom" for women.[1] That bit of equalizing has translated into a lot of underdressed girls with absurd expectations being fed beer after beer by frat boys. Allowing women to believe that the workplace was as enviable as they'd fantasized just means a lot less time to load the washing machine with the pile of laundry feminism failed to shrink to a more manageable size. Even suffrage looks troublingly silly from certain angles. The female vote goes largely toward asking the government to please provide what a man traditionally gave a woman, in the days when the wide exercise of Christian norms resulted in men actually sticking around. Where's that cosmic switch? Should we jiggle it back and forth a few times and hope for improvement?

---

[1] If we want to get historically technical about who took rape seriously and when, it was in the enlightened year of 1977—well into the establishment of feminist thought in the American mind—that the Supreme Court ruled against the last state law that permitted the Old Testament practice of punishing rape with the death penalty.

Cosmic, of course, means "of the world." Again, that's not us. Christians have seen what the world has to offer. Recently, its great ideas have included banning certain words on the rationale that women are so vulnerable as to be crippled by adjectives, and allowing children to decide whether they are boys or girls regardless of biological evidence. That is how we are also able to see that the changeless Word of God is the one trustworthy standard by which we can live. The world *can't* keep up with the relentless progression of its own bad ideas. For example:

> Does pornography exploit women or offer them a powerful professional opportunity?

> What happens when your same-sex domestic partner tells you that she's realized she's transsexual and will be having her body retooled into the kind you *didn't* want to sleep next to?

> Shouldn't we impose hiring quotas on trash collectors and plumbers so women are more fairly represented in those trades, and require more men to be employed as early childhood educators and manicurists?

> Are male soldiers allowed to clobber female combatants in opposing militaries, or does that qualify as the world's last taboo, violence against women?

But the Church *won't* keep up with advances so backward. The people of God always appear to be on some wrong side of history from a human perspective. Running afoul of human "wisdom" can be awkward or even dangerous. But the believer knows it is far more dangerous to be on the wrong side of the God of history. It can never be wise to live counter to the wisdom of the world's maker.

History is written by the victors, so we need some way to judge those victors and their version of events. The iconic movie *The Matrix* stages the philosophical thought experiment of the *brain in a vat*. The idea is that being completely enclosed within a system prevents knowledge that the system exists. If a brain in a vat receives the same kind of stimuli as a brain in a skull, the vat-brain can't tell that it's in a vat and not a skull. Living by the timeless Word of God is our protection against being brains in the vat of history when we happen to have landed. All times have their problems, and ours is no exception. If we must be products of our time, we would do well to remember that eventually these will be remembered as the bad old days too.

Brains for Women!

Why does God give women brains? It's a question you may have found occasion to ask at some point in your life, especially if you share a bathroom with members of the male species. *If I'm doomed to clean other people's pee off toilets forever, why do I have to know exactly how disgusting it is? If I quit, would we all die of filth? If I don't, will I kill everybody?*

Not to get personal, but you are a pragmatist. You value things for their practical application, including yourself. You look at your set of skills and abilities and consider them wasted if you don't use them to their fullest extent, out there in the "real world," and probably also for monetary compensation.

But what does Scripture say? "I praise You, for I am fearfully and wonderfully made" (Psalm 139:14), *not* fearfully and wonderfully useful. Your aptitudes are *who* God has made you, in addition to being tools He has given you to use. Their application is not more valuable than the testimony your unique existence gives to His creative power. So first of all, you are smart, skilled, and virtuous because you are a work of God, not because He needed a sculptor, an engineer, or a teacher down here to straighten things out.

For Adam, no suitable helper was found. A heifer wasn't good enough. The man needed someone corresponding to him. What's good for the gander is a goose, that is, someone who can fly, honk, float, *and* (under the right set of circumstances) give him a gosling. So second, women were made by God to match men, who are almost certainly human.

Let's get messier, though. To a certain extent, people see through pragmatism's weaker arguments; for example, most women are willing to trade their unstretchmarked stomachs to have children. But to completely give up the protections pragmatism offers our pride is difficult. *If I'm this smart, don't I deserve an advanced degree?* Or more cunningly, *Isn't it bad stewardship for me not to cultivate and make use of my talents? For the glory of God, of course?*

Our first order of business in dealing with this question is to remember that there is an office in the Church that allows both men and women to make full use of their publicly relevant talents: celibacy. The person who never marries remains free of the constraints that come with marriage and family, which will likely mean a vastly diminished amount of toilet cleaning. Everything is a trade-off, and freedom is the counterbalance to companionship when the benefits of celibacy and marriage are contrasted. This paragraph is pretty short for the size of the decision it describes, but that's kind of the point. Not getting married bypasses a world of complications and challenges to piety. Celibacy should be seriously considered by any woman who can't see herself dealing with the contention that naturally arises when a male and a female try to get along for a lifetime. There, you've been warned.

What about the married? Their calling to love their neighbors as themselves requires them to understand clearly who their neighbors are. The word itself contains the answer. Our *neighb*ors are those who are *nigh*, which means *near*, to us. No one is nearer to us than the people in our own households. We are their servants before we are any other person's.

So what about those times in life when many of us find ourselves devoured by the mindless tasks of basic neighborly care? Are women being bad stewards during years of issuing Muppets bandages instead of performing surgery, or negotiating Lego-sharing rather than drafting contracts? Are a woman's gifts being wasted if her attendance to one sick person leaves her with no energy to reopen that barely started master's thesis? When Grandpa can't take care of himself anymore, is his daughter wasting her talents by being there for him instead of with the people who used to be her co-workers? What if *every one* of these scenarios played out in a lady's life; would she have failed from start to finish at making use of her gifts?

O pragmatist, what are your gifts? Just ask someone who can't do something. Ask a hungry child if the making of breakfast is a big deal. Ask an amputee how he feels about having to rely on someone else to take out his trash. Ask someone who can't keep up with her dog anymore if she misses using her pooper scooper on a cold day. Ask a person who can't turn in bed how much she likes having other people do it for her.

When we speak of our gifts, we always mean the impressive ones. We're concerned with preserving our opportunities to do the things we enjoy. We like to be good at something, and we like to have other people notice and tell us we're good at it. We identify ourselves with the activities we like rather than those necessary to life. A librarian is probably happier with her orderly books than her disorderly nephews; an actuary would most likely rather count beans than cook them for supper. This requires that life meet us on our terms. We want to get married when the fancy strikes us, no sooner and certainly no later. We want a certain number of children during a certain time frame. We want our working or not working, whichever we prefer, to be what is best for our family. We want everyone to be independent because having to deal with a dependent person can keep us from leaving the house whenever we want. We make virtue out of necessity, and necessity out of everything, so that none of our decisions can ever be criticized. Somewhere along this path, our pious concern for being good stewards of gifts and talents becomes indistinguishable from our pride and comfort.

The joke is on us, and it isn't even a funny one. The sin-rotted world we will always have with us in this life, but it needs us a lot less than we like to tell ourselves. Maybe you sing like Diana Damrau, run Germany like Angela Merkel, or discover francium like Marguerite Perey. Or maybe you're just a regular chick, in which case it might be a little easier to see that lots of people can sing. Lots of people can run Germany. Lots of people can die horrible deaths for the sake of science. And they will. But no one else can be to her neighbors (remembering what that word means) the neighbor God has made it her station to be. The closer two people are, the less irreplaceable they are to each other. A married woman is her husband's only wife. A mother is the only one her children have. No parents have so many daughters that they wouldn't miss one of them if she disappeared from their life. The person who knows just how lonely the old maid next door feels is that lady's lifeline to a day with a little bit of human sunshine.

None of the titles that go with those jobs—Wife, Mom, Daughter, Friend—are as impressive as Operatic Soprano or Chancellor or Chemist of Major Historical Significance. But each of them stands for at least one person who has a real, time-consuming claim on us. God gave those people to us; *they* are gifts, and a person is worth a lot more than being awesome at Hula-Hooping (even Hula-Hooping for Christ). Personally serving the people we have received as gifts from God is something we can always do in good conscience. No one can ever regret the unimpeachable good she has done her nighest neighbors by supporting them in body and life as only a good neighbor can. More often than not, that service means boring—if not exactly brainless—stuff.

So sure, we would do anything for God, like get eaten by lions and all that. But He asks His people to live boring and unnoticeable lives for Him more often than He calls out the lions. He has given us a standing order: "Do nothing from selfish ambition or conceit, but in humility count others more significant than yourselves. Let each of you look not only to his own interests, but also to the interests of others" (Philippians 2:3–4). Dr. Thomas Winger says in his commentary on Ephesians, "We are not free to choose which consequences of the Gospel we would like for our lives." He is speaking of St. Paul, whose commitment to the Gospel landed the apostle in prison. But most of us find that life in the Gospel leads merely to crises of dumb stuff we don't feel like doing. The brainiest of women may well be called upon to give up a promotion, a degree, a paycheck, or just the freedom to go to the store whenever because some miserable person would be less miserable if she were more available.

The devil, the world, and our flesh will do their impeachingest when these crises arise, and there is no more insidious lie than that business about stewardship. In his novel *Bleak House*, Charles Dickens includes a memorable character named Mrs. Jellyby. This fine lady spends all her time working for the cause of Borrioboola-Gha, an African village in need of bettering by its betters, which she of course is. While she pours herself into her noble task, her children go dirty, hungry, and unhelped through problems of all kinds. This is what the devil would have for all of our loved ones. He wants us to think it is better for us to "use our brains" or even "serve the Church" than wipe down the toilets of those no-good jerks we live with, not to mention whatever other nasty things they need done.

The truth is that our fun and flashy gifts are the icing on the cake of living at a higher level of comfort than most people in history. Pursuing and monetizing one's interests is a totally unnecessary dessert after a healthy meal of basic physical wellness and met needs, and just eating icing will eventually make us every bit as sick as never cleaning the toilets. Even secular sociologists say there is no better way to serve society than taking care of one's own family. This is the most important task on anyone's stewardship list. If you're a gourmet chef cooking for your family every night, your family is exceedingly blessed. What is the world to you anyway, with all its vaunted diners? We all want the best for our loved ones. How sad it would be if we failed to share with them that special gift we consider the best of ourselves.

Why does God give women brains? Because He gives all people brains for His glory and the good of His people, starting with the stinky-footed one watching YouTube on the couch, or the old one who camps in what used to be your dining room, or the little ones asleep down the hall, or the local mob of His infuriating elect who have never noticed that you keep the candelabras polished. Go on, thank Him. And then figure out what you've got to do for everybody tomorrow, whoever your "everybody" may be. It might not be impressive, but it does take a brain.

BRIDEZILLA OF CHRIST

My dad was a parish pastor for over twenty years. Presiding at weddings was not his favorite thing. It's not that Dad was antimatrimony. He has been enjoying a blessed marriage himself for thirty-five-plus years. What Dad opposed was weddings. Technically, that's not even it. He was opposed to the culturally prescribed trappings and selfish obsessions that often (not *always*) soured those occasions.

One afternoon, Dad spoke plainly on this point. I was probably about twelve years old. He came home on a Saturday and I started asking questions. You know, the usual.

What was the bride's dress like? How about her hair? the veil? What colors were the bridesmaids wearing? What kind of flowers? Where was the reception? Was there going to be a dance? Did you see the cake? How long did the photographs take? In other words, how did the bride do in planning her big day?

Dad explained to me that none of those things mattered to him. They weren't unimportant to him because he was a guy or because he was a grump. Those things were unimportant. Period. My questions were focused on the wedding stuff that mattered least. I was most interested in the activities that actually distracted from the heart of the day.

TLC, MTV, and others confirm that there are many, many people in our society who major in the distractions. One show awards prizes to brides who put on the best weddings. This is determined based on the following categories: best dress, best food, best venue, and best overall experience—which is to say, the guests had fun. The bride who does the best job wins the big prize. Another show documents the details of a bride's agonizing quest to finally say "Yes!" in that magical moment. But the show is not interested in the yes that is included in the marriage vows. Rather, the obsession that will hold an audience's attention is over the "'yes' to the dress." Then there's the show that popularized the title *bridezilla*. Without providing a definition, most readers will know precisely what this means. Bridezillas don't beam or blush. Bridezillas bellow, bark, and berate. It's understood to be a bad thing, but it still proves hard to avoid. "I don't want to be a bridezilla, but . . . " Any sentence that starts like that almost certainly indicates the bride has, in fact, become a bit of a monster.

To steer clear of bridezilla territory and the fire-breathing entailments, a bride is called away from self-enamorment. This is a good thing. It provides rest and peace where there is otherwise taxing work and endless fretting. There's great joy in the knowledge that the wedding day and, thereafter, the marriage are about being loved by the one who chose her. That man who asked her to marry him? Yeah, that guy. It's about being loved by him not just on the night of the proposal, or the day of the wedding, but for a lifetime. For all of the activity that is involved in wedding preparation, the ultimate posture of a bride is one of passivity. This remembrance and focus make it possible to release all the little self-absorptions that lead to tantrums of one kind or another that end in the unbecoming phrase, "It's my day!"

It *is* the bride's day, but it isn't her job to put on a memorable show and make herself look good. It's not about how well she coordinated her dress with those of her bridesmaids. It's not about how meticulously her meal was planned or her cake was decorated or her party favors were personalized or her music was selected. It is her time to be loved and cherished. That is what makes her the star. The big day is about who she is. It's about whom she will be with for as long as they both shall live. The focus is on the "yes" of the wedding vows. It is on the promise made to her by her groom, who pledges to love, honor, and keep her, to have and to hold her, for as long as they both shall live. When the bride is thinking less of the external frills, she can think more of the godly vocation that awaits her as one who will receive and also give love without condition.

When this is the wedding day portrait, it serves well as a picture of Christ and His Bride, the Church, as described in Ephesians 5:22–33. We embody this understanding of bridehood not as something we do, but as someone we are. We are Christ's elect by grace (Romans 8:33). He chose us. Our love for Him is foremost and forever grounded in His everlasting love for us.

As a wedding day and marital focus are centered around a promise, so, too, is the life of the Bride of Christ. We come to worship every Sunday to hear again that promise made to us by Christ, the perfect groom. Nothing will separate us from His love (Romans 8:38–39). Each church service functions as a vow renewal of that sure Word.

When we gather to worship, the point is not to show off how good we look or what awesome things we have done. The point is to delight in His will and what He has done for us. We receive more of the Groom's good gifts—His fore-tastes of the feast to come. We are not there to plan the meal or even to serve it to ourselves. We are there to be fed and be forgiven.

Christ has also promised to return in glory, and He's tak-en care of all that planning too. Our posture is one of pas-sivity again. He will dress us with a robe of righteousness (Revelation 6:11). He has prepared the banquet (Psalm 23:5). The venue is the promised land, which is His work and His doing (John 14:2–3). And as for the overall experience, it will be divine!

Life in the new creation isn't about an eternity of our personal sound track or our favorite food or our preferred guest list. Life in the new creation is about being with our Lord, who loves us perfectly. When we're there, we will final-ly be able to love Him perfectly too.

For now and for all of time, being the Bride of Christ is about being joined to Him and cleaving to Him. That one-ness with Him is what makes us blush and beam. Here below we blush in the knowledge that He should love us so dearly without any merit or worthiness in us. There in eter-nity we will beam in the light of consummate joy, which will last for as long as we both shall live—forever.

Not Fair

Once upon a time, the world operated on the basis of reality. The men hauled logs and the women wove fabric, and nobody called upon Captain Obvious to explain why. Doubtless there were women who disliked weaving and men who disliked hauling logs, but liking had nothing to do with it. There was work to be done and the determination of who did what went like this: *Whoever is stronger will do the heavy and dangerous stuff. Whoever's not will do the other stuff. Whoever has babies will take care of them.*

Guys are strong; at least, they're stronger than most girls. Girls have babies; at least, many of them do, and guys never do. If a guy and a girl each decided that the other was worth having, they also took on all the work their life together created. In most cases, this found the girl home with babies and the guy out at work to keep them fed and warm. If a girl found herself with a baby and no guy, she was in trouble.

Now, upon our time, people are not okay with this. The setup is plainly, ridiculously unfair. What it comes down to is that an act equally committed has totally unequal consequences. One party's life is changed forever while the other might never even learn about it. The solution we have proposed is a work-around, as H. L. Mencken foretold in 1918: "What these virtuous bel dames actually desire in their hearts is not that the male be reduced to chemical purity, but that the franchise of dalliance be extended to themselves." Girls can enjoy the sexual libertinism available to guys by means of drugs and doohickeys. Babies, the perpetual flies in the ointment of human awesomeness, have become entirely optional, as have their attendant problems.

So now the world operates according to an ideal: everybody should get to do whatever they want all the time. Sack-hopping without consequence is open to all, either by nature or artifice. If you want to be married, you should be married to someone who makes you feel amazing. Do things you love, realize your potential, never forget how beautiful you are. Or else!

The assumption fueling this ideal, again, is unfairness. It refuses to accept that it has written an impossible equation by insisting that Female=Male. Moreover, it has forgotten how equations work. It never imagines that the costs of being female are balanced out by a commensurate benefit.

The F=M ideal cannot see how a husband who gives all his productive energy for the needs of his family is as noble as the guy who runs out on a girl he's impregnated is reprehensible. F=M fails to understand that having a baby under the right circumstances is as sublime as having one under the wrong circumstances is dire. F=M can't see that every trouble, trial, and danger of motherhood is more than repaid in the bottomless eyes of the mortal immortal born of it. And it is here we begin to see that things *are* unfair, but not because they are a swindle. They are unfair because they are a divinely generous overpayment.

God is not out to get women for their nasty womanliness. He has given to them the possibility of a life's work so gratifying and lasting as to present us with two difficulties. The first is seeing how things are fair to men. For all the world's talk about "making a difference," very little of this is accomplished in public life or the market. Nearly all work that goes on in the world is subsistence or maintenance. Discovery, invention, and revolution are an infinitesimal percentage of humanity's workday. A company must be kept afloat long enough for its owner to retire; a war must be fought as evidence of an ongoing need for a military; a lab or firm or practice or school must stay open so that it will stay open. We must train up and employ the next generation so that it can train up and employ the next generation. A provider absorbs all the indignity, boredom, and futility of these circular enterprises because folks gotta eat.

Those ever-eating folks are what matter, and they didn't turn up out of nowhere. Every human life is a monument to another human's work, and that second human is always a woman. She may have done nothing more than gestate and deliver a baby, but even that work is rather magnificent. In truth, most mothers stick with their children far beyond nine months and a rough day. So the second difficulty is understanding how the world has succeeded in making this work into a punishment, a joke, or a sidebar to the "real" things that supposedly matter in a woman's life.

It is both the wide availability and the arbitrary unavailability of marriage and motherhood that demand that they be diminished. A poor, ugly, unintellectual, or insignificant woman can be a wonderful wife and mother. A rich, beautiful, ingenious, or highborn woman may find herself jilted or barren. This is intolerable to the world, where beauty and worth can and must be measured and rewarded. Female domesticity cannot be explained or controlled, so it must be humiliated.

Humiliation is merely putting a cruel twist upon what is humble, and the domestic vocation is thoroughly humble. It is no difficult task to persuade people that hard and unacclaimed things aren't worth doing. The tasks that fall to wives and mothers are repetitive and unglamorous, which is precisely what makes them hard. No one is impressed seeing a woman pick up damp socks every day; much less are they impressed by not seeing it. She plods on, unseen at work designed to go unnoticed (people only notice when it *doesn't* get done). She is easily led to believe that what she is doing is not appreciated and does not matter. Her temptation is to imagine that her lot is worse than that of the man whose labors are usually no more gratifying but who still gives her what he earns for them.

This returns us to our first difficulty: what reward God has to offer the man, who can claim only the smallest technicality of life-giving and none of the transcendence. In fact, it is this lack of transcendence that makes male domesticity at least as confounding to the world as the female variety. The man who voluntarily commits himself to a woman, giving her everything that is his and forsaking all others, is seen as a bland fool. But as a wife who knows the true value of her work is untouched by the world's accusation of inadequacy, the husband who knows his work understands that he is richer than the baron with his harem, wiser than the free-spirit junkie with his expanded mind. His reward is the clear conscience won by integrity. The faithful husband knows how easily he could walk out and how little he could live with himself if he did. At the end of the day, at the end of his life, at the end of the world, he has kept his word.

The modern and postmodern eras betray their true natures with their inability to see that what is best in life is always a product of sacrifice, discipline, and perseverance. Crying about fairness is a five-year-old's way of handling realities perceived as unpleasant, and the world's solutions are just as immature. Contemporary wisdom levels the playing field by cutting a leg off every player. It has tried to make everyone equal by enabling all of us to be as bad as the worst person.

It's not fair, but how could it be? The division of humanity into male and female is, Robert Farrar Capon tells us, "the marvelous bargain by which we get two species for the price of one."[2] Men make life possible, and women make life livable. A good woman triumphs by embracing what she is bound to without resentment, receiving what she is given with humility and gratitude. A good man triumphs by embracing what he is not bound to, rather than creating the world of pain within his power. What is clear is that neither of us could do without the other. Marriage surely multiplies two people's troubles. The outsized payoff is that our gracious God causes its blessings to increase not arithmetically, but exponentially. Reality being what it is, people of sound mind may observe that although liking has nothing to do with it, loving could only help.

[2] Robert Farrar Capon, *Bed and Board: Plain Talk about Marriage* (New York: Simon and Schuster, 1965), 48.

The Real Winners
of the Sexual Revolution

The sexual revolution, like any war, had winners and losers.

Women were out to win something really important. It was their big chance to assert their libido and secure their freedom in the bedroom, on the big screen, billboards, and everywhere.

Thanks to the battles so bravely fought, women can have sex without the commitment of marriage. Women can use birth control. Women can wear short skirts and tight shirts. Women can post Internet pics of themselves wearing no more (but possibly less) than undergarments. Women can have one-night stands and multiple partners and all the rest. Women can flaunt "it" however they want.

Those were the outcomes of the revolution.

You do understand who the real winners were, don't you?

Right. Moving on.

Submission: Impossible?

S ubmission?' That's a bad word. Doesn't that mean a wife has to do whatever her husband says—that he's some kind of dictator, and she's basically his slave?"

It doesn't mean that.

"Okay, but I know it's just some old-timey notion that doesn't apply today."

Wrong. It still applies.

"Oh, great. So this is a way that men get to lord it over women and use the Bible to justify their actions."

Again, no. Have you been talking to any serpents recently, by chance?

"No. Why?"

You're willing to allow something other than the Scriptures to define things for you. The definition you're working with makes God's design and order sound awful. If submission is something that God set up, do you think it is a bad thing?

"Well . . . no. I suppose not."

Who might have an interest in making God's arrangement sound disagreeable? Who would want to make you think you'd really be better off ignoring God's system?

"What are you getting at?"

If you are trying to wiggle out of a system that God clearly established in His Word, if you feel that God's setup is cruel and unloving, if you compare your culture's modus operandi with the Bible, and the biblical stance is the one that's not working for you . . . well, maybe someone's gotten inside your head to lead you astray.

"So you're trying to tell me that I'm possessed if I don't want to be a slave to my husband, chained to the stove?"

Uh . . . no. Why so defensive? The Bible never describes a situation where a wife is a slave to her husband, required to cater to his every whim. That's not what submission means, according to the Scriptures.

"Okay. So what does it mean?"

Good Lutheran question. Now you're talking! We'll look at the text that gets everyone in a bunch. Ephesians 5:22–33 says:

> Wives, submit to your own husbands, as to
> the Lord. For the husband is the head of the
> wife even as Christ is the head of the church,
> His body, and is Himself its Savior. Now as the
> church submits to Christ, so also wives should
> submit in everything to their husbands. Hus-
> bands, love your wives, as Christ loved the
> church and gave Himself up for her, that He
> might sanctify her, having cleansed her by
> the washing of water with the word, so that
> He might present the church to Himself in
> splendor, without spot or wrinkle or any such
> thing, that she might be holy and without
> blemish. In the same way husbands should
> love their wives as their own bodies. He
> who loves his wife loves himself. For no one
> ever hated his own flesh, but nourishes and

cherishes it, just as Christ does the church, because we are members of His body. "Therefore a man shall leave his father and mother and hold fast to his wife, and the two shall become one flesh." This mystery is profound, and I am saying that it refers to Christ and the church. However, let each one of you love his wife as himself, and let the wife see that she respects her husband.

The model for submission here is our Lord Jesus Christ, and His Bride, the Church. Starting with that picture, do you think of Christ as the kind of husband who chains His wife to the stove? Does He demand that she refill beer mugs whilst He watches football all afternoon?

"No."

Okay. Why not?

"Because He's never described like that in the Gospels."

Exactly. Christ and the Church provide the model for submission. Do you think that Christ being the Head, the one who leads, is a bad thing?

"No. That's a rather good thing."

A very good thing! Does He seem like a domineering tyrant who bosses people around and never listens to what they think or want?

"No. The Gospels are full of people coming up to Him and asking for help, and He listens and helps. Even when the disciples make some pretty boneheaded mistakes, He continues to forgive and teach them."

Yes. See? You really know your stuff when you get past the defensive liberation routine! People who describe "submission" as a twisted system whereby men bark commands and women shuffle about servilely have it all wrong. This is not consistent with the picture we have of Christ. What's more, Jesus tells His disciples that they are to lead in the way He leads. Consider Matthew 20:25–28:

> Jesus called them to Him and said, "You know that the rulers of the Gentiles lord it over them, and their great ones exercise authority over them. It shall not be so among you. But whoever would be great among you must be your servant, and whoever would be first among you must be your slave, even as the Son of Man came not to be served but to serve, and to give His life as a ransom for many."

The model of leadership that Jesus lives, and tells His disciples to lead, is one of service. Even though Christ is God, the Second Person of the Trinity, He took on flesh and came to serve humanity—most significantly by being crucified and rising three days later. He does not "lord it over" people, even though He is *the* Lord.

This is the example for a man in his marriage. As Christ talked with, listened to, and answered the prayers of those around Him, so also a husband will talk to, listen to, and respond to the requests of his wife.

"That sounds pretty good, but I still don't like the idea of him having the final word. I have my own ideas, you know, and they're really good. Why should he get to do the thinking for both of us?"

You probably take orders from other folks who aren't

your husband and I bet it doesn't bother you. There are lots of other people doing the thinking for you, and you smile and nod and get in line.

"What do you mean?"

Has a doctor ever told you to eat less sodium or get a flu shot? Has a teacher ever told you to sign a form? Has a boss ever told you to get to work by 8 a.m.? Has the government ever posted a speed limit sign or demanded a percentage of your income? Has a Web site ever told you to start using coconut oil, like, yesterday?

"Of course."

In all of those cases, you probably did what you were told without too much foot dragging or whining. You probably didn't feel disrespected or devalued.

"Well, yes, but that's different. Those people are in positions of authority, and those rules are for my good and the good of others."

Right. That's exactly what I'm getting at. God established authority for our good. He has done so in the Church, in society, and also in families. How much more when the husband you chose makes a recommendation or determination should you expect that it would be for your good? Don't you think it will be grounded in his love for you? Those others don't have any personal interest in you. Your husband does! He's your sweetheart, your soul mate, your best friend, your other half, your happy ending . . .

Did I find your term for the relationship yet?

"Ha-ha, yes."

Okay, so you see, he's a really special person. And yet, you were all huffy about submitting to the person you love most and to whom you have voluntarily bound yourself on that basis.

"Oh. Okay, my husband can have the final word. He's a good guy. But what about people who abuse this? What about men who abuse their wives—emotionally or even physically—and use 'submission' as their justification?"

It's sin. Remember, Christ is the example. Does He emotionally or physically abuse His Bride, the Church?

"No."

Of course not. Now, obviously *we* are not perfect as He is. The world is full of sinners. Human spouses sin. Very sadly, some sin in ways like emotional and physical abuse, and some twist the Word of God to justify their sinful actions. These are terrible things that should not happen. They should be repented of and stopped.

But their sins, while very wrong, do not invalidate the good order and design that God established at the beginning. Submission is part of the order. The Father is the Head of Christ, Christ is the Head of the Church, the husband is the head of the wife. There is submission in all of these relationships, and it is not culturally irrelevant, abusive, cruel, passé, or whatever other bad name the devil wants to try and stick to it.

It is a beautiful description of God and how He set up His creation—of how Christ cares for and loves His Bride so that she may be presented to Him in splendor, without spot or wrinkle or any such thing, that she might be holy and without blemish.

"It doesn't sound so bad when you put it like *that*."

Oh, that's not how I put it. That's how God put it. *Submission* isn't a bad word. It's God's Word. We cool?

The More, the Merrier?

One of the dreariest news items we've all gotten used to hearing is the one about decreasing church membership. This decrease concerns and troubles us. We understand that eternal election is buried in the hiddenness of God and there are limits to our understanding. Nevertheless, we care. An increase in the population of the Kingdom, the family of God, is something we hope for, pray for, and work for, while acknowledging that it is God alone who grants growth.

When new members join a congregation, whether through Baptism or adult confirmation, there is great rejoicing. We give thanks for another child of God—another son or daughter of the King. We thank God for another sibling in the faith—another brother or sister in Christ. We pray for more.

As those conversations are taking place, though, conversations about increasing the size of individual families are not happening. Luther's commentary on this issue is quite good: "From the first chapter of Genesis [1:28] comes this sentiment about children: 'God blessed them.' He says 'Blessed' and expects you to respond with 'Thanks be to God,' but this is generally forgotten."[3]

---

[3] Luther's Works, volume 54, page 59.

We affirm together a resounding "Thanks be to God!" to the growing of the family of God. But when it comes to the growing of families, we say, "Not necessarily," or "Only if it's convenient," or "Sure, if that's your thing." Although we earnestly and rightly pray for the Lord to cause greater and greater growth in the Church, that talk doesn't transfer when we move beyond the family of God into the homes of godly families.

Scripture speaks clearly about children and families (Psalm 68:6; 127; 128; Proverbs 18:22; Malachi 2:15; Matthew 18:10; Mark 9:37). But we in the Church are saying virtually nothing.

There are a few explanations for why it is so quiet. Our primary teachers of the faith are men, and men may not feel comfortable taking on a topic with distinctly feminine implications. The conversation can be hurtful to our brothers and sisters who are unable to have any (or any more) children due to painful crosses that they bear. Less diplomatic approaches to this topic are always off-putting. Perhaps it's also because we're sinners and we're selfish and we don't want to talk or hear about this. Maybe we're afraid of what it might mean for us.

Whatever the reason, a large segment of the Church is essentially silent while society speaks loudly on this topic. Only the Roman Catholic Church still speaks definitively about God's giving of children in Christian marriage, although evidence indicates that the message is not received any better there than it is among the general population. Christian families are taking their talking points from a secular message board that does not faithfully represent the Word and will of the Lord.

Society says that women (and men) should think first of what they want out of life. Children will interfere with those pursuits. Financial security and job satisfaction and trips to Tuscany should be our top priorities. Society says that children come at a high price. Even beyond the obvious monetary costs of raising a child, there are population concerns to consider,[4] annoyances to be dealt with, sacrifices to be made, and a great number of other things that make people wonder why anyone ever had kids in the first place. The fruitful womb in our time and culture is considered a curious anomaly at best. More likely, it is an object of criticism or ridicule.

Our ancient mothers in the faith (and fathers, for that matter) prized the fruitful womb *not* as a result of their time or culture. They did so because they were Christian. They understood that children are blessings, and that blessings are desired, prayed for, and treasured. When the Lord caused the womb to bear in abundance, they rejoiced. When a womb did not bear, they mourned. This attitude conformed

---

[4] In their response to the Augsburg Confession, the Roman Catholics argued that priests and monks should remain celibate because the earth had been filled! This was in the year 1530, when the earth's total population was around 500 million. Philip Melanchthon replied: "They say that in the beginning, the commandment was given to populate the earth. Now that the earth has been populated, marriage is not commanded. See how wisely they judge! Human nature is so formed by God's Word that it is fruitful not only in the beginning of creation, but as long as this nature of our bodies exists. Humanity is fruitful just as the earth becomes fruitful by the Word, 'Let the earth sprout vegetation, plants yielding seed' (Genesis 1:11). Because of this ordinance, the earth not only started to produce plants in the beginning, but as long as this natural order exists, the fields are covered every year. Therefore, just as human laws cannot change the nature of the earth, so, without God's special work, neither vows nor a human law can change a human being's nature" (Apology of the Augsburg Confession, Article XXIII, paragraph 8).

to the will of God for His creation. *Be fruitful and multiply.* That commission was issued without any expiration date.

But the twentieth century brought sad conflict into the Christian Church on this topic of procreation. Propagation of the human race requires a staggering amount of suffering and sacrifice from those who carry it out. The general consensus is that it would be absurd to hope for, pray for, and receive this line of blessings without measure.

In spite of this, a multitude of tacky cross-stitch patterns will not allow us to forget that children are a blessing. Scripture is equally insistent on the point. While the ethical details will probably confound and divide the children of God for what remains of our earthly time, there are a few things of which we may be certain:

When a child is brought to His font of rebirth, the Lord and Giver of life never looks at that baby and groans, "Another one?" No. He is pleased to see His handiwork—knit together in the womb with care—receive the promise of eternal life.

The Holy Trinity and undivided Unity, the essence of self-giving and all-creating Love, sees not another college tuition or carbon footprint, but another saint bought with Christ's holy, precious blood and with His innocent suffering and death.

Failing to confess this truth in its entirety is an act of unfaithfulness to God and Scripture. The children of God cannot lead holy lives when the Word of God is not taught in truth and purity. It's an insult to be told, "You can't handle the truth!" Women don't want to be patronized. Avoiding topics that might not be well received is refusing to treat someone like a reasonable adult. It is particularly unhelpful to women who would welcome more children if only everyone hadn't lectured them about how irresponsible that would be.

The fear of causing pain also drives the Church's reluctance to uphold scriptural teaching on children. When the dear ones in our midst who are unable to have children (or more children) hear that children are a blessing, it only validates the pain they already bear, and in which they feel so alone. But the Church can better care for these members by rightly acknowledging the depth of their pain and loss. Then these precious brothers and sisters will hear the truth (that children are a blessing—which they already know—hence their deep sorrow), but they will finally receive a word of love as well.

There is some Law to be found in this conversation. But the Law of God is good and wise even though it is not easy, and we cannot know what is good and wise without it (Psalm 19:12).[5] Moreover, there is a tremendous amount of blessing, Gospel, and grace. By not having the conversation, everyone is missing out on both. "It is written in Genesis [33:5] with reference to children, 'Those whom God has graciously given to me,' as in the psalm [119:29], 'Graciously teach me thy law.'"[6]

---

[5] While we're thinking about the Law, let's hear from St. Augustine: "Freedom occurs when we delight in the Law of God, for freedom gives you joy. As long as you do what is right out of fear, you find no delight in God. Find your delight in Him, and you are free." Lectures or Tractates on the Gospel according to St. John; Tractate XLI.10 quoted in Treasury of Daily Prayer (St. Louis: Concordia, 2010), 387.

[6] Luther's Works, volume 54, page 59.

There is a selfish, sinful old Adam or Eve in all of us who would rather not deal with what God has to say about children and family. But the Church is not a PTA meeting or an office party. Some conversations are hard. Some words of truth are hard. That doesn't mean they shouldn't be had or said.

The Church is our true home and the growth of the Church is a blessing we are always eager to receive. Therein rests the lesson for our own homes. We give thanks for another child of God—another son or daughter of the King. We pray for more. Let's give thanks for another child in a Christian home—another son or daughter. Let's pray for more.

DEBORAH VS. SHE-RA: EXCEPTION VS. RULE

In 1985, youngsters met a new cartoon heroine: She-Ra, Princess of Power. Like most superheroes, she was a force for good and not for evil. She reserved her famous body-throws for moments of obliged defense, not antagonistic offense. All this she did "for the honor of Grayskull," according to her transforming tagline. The fact that she was a sword-wielding, rock-hurling, robot-destroying lady may have seemed a bit unladylike, but desperate times called for desperate measures.

Everyone's favorite biblical heroine, Deborah, knew all about desperate times and measures. Deborah was a judge. Judges were appointed to lead, defend, and deliver Israel from their enemies. Like superheroes, they were faced with fearful challenges. Also, like comic-book stars, they were quite often the underdogs.

The people of Israel repeatedly landed themselves in trouble of one kind or another, so "then the Lord raised up judges, who saved them out of the hand of those who plundered them" (Judges 2:16). The deliverers of this period were all beset with an obvious worldly weakness. The Lord didn't pick the strongest and smartest He-Man of the bunch. He consistently chose the human equivalent of Mighty Mouse.

Othniel was nothing but a famous guy's kid brother. Ehud was left-handed, which got a big thumbs-down from the military tactics of that day. Gideon came from the weakest clan and was a nobody in his father's feeble house. Jephthah was an ill-reputed son of a prostitute, disowned by his own family, whose modest qualification consisted of having gathered together a band of reportedly "worthless fellows" (Judges 11:3). Samson? That bloke was strong, as everyone knows, but he was also a womanizer, a rotten judge of character, and an arrogant hothead. He had problems.

What was Deborah's weakness? She wasn't weak-willed. She wasn't a coward. She wasn't a show-off. She wasn't bossy. She was determined, faithful, loyal, and strong. Actually, Deborah sounds like a great candidate, but how does this fit with the theme of the judges being chosen *in spite* of their weakness, not because of their strengths? All of the other judges were obviously ignoble or ill-bred, but Deborah actually sounds like a surefire shoo-in!

What made Deborah unlikely for this calling was her womanhood. Where the man from the very beginning had been created to lead and protect the woman, Deborah's military involvement was a clear and surprising departure from that created order established in Genesis and confirmed and esteemed in Ephesians 5.

For the judges' victories to be seen quite clearly as not theirs but the Lord's, each person had to be unsuited to play the part. Where She-Ra battled for the honor of Grayskull, Deborah was called upon to fight for the honor of the one true God. Deborah understood that her role as deliverer was not meant to prove that she was the ultimate biblical

Wonder Woman, but to show that she was a regular woman and, therefore, not qualified for the violent and valiant task before her. Her natural *dis*qualifications would secure the recognition that the Lord was the true Deliverer.

Under normal circumstances, the mothers of the living are not called upon to take life. Violence and killing, even when justified, are contrary to the intrinsic qualities of women, who are called upon to protect and care for the weakest members of society. With this battle, the Lord was not establishing a new norm for women in front-line military combat. Rather, with the surprising defeat of Sisera, the Lord demonstrated how Deborah and tent-peg-driving Jael were the *exceptions* that proved the rule. Precisely because they weren't cut out for weapon wielding, they were used as improbable instruments in humble service to the real Deliverer.

She-Ra, Princess of Power, fought bravely in her very short skirt and her fancy gold crown. Along came Xena, Warrior Princess, with her flowing dark locks and her scary good looks. Finally, society was ready for G. I. Jane, who dispensed with the princess business altogether and became like a man in every way possible to prove her combatant qualifications. The problem with all of these gals was that, unlike Deborah and Jael, they were eventually regarded more as a fine, unqualified rule than the obvious exception thereto.

She-Ra, Xena, Jane, and their iconic ilk are fictional, of course, but their make-believe battling paved the way to a standard for real life. There is now an effort to endorse women in combat and promote "equal opportunities" for males and females on the front lines of warfare.

What would Deborah say to all of this? She'd probably say that it was unnatural for and unbecoming of a woman to march to the front lines.[7] In fact, this is what she said. The Lord actually told a man, Barak, to go out and face the enemy army. God even promised victory! Deborah reminded Barak of this assignment. Barak, though, was afraid. "Barak said to her, 'If you will go with me, I will go, but if you will not go with me, I will not go' " (Judges 4:8).

Deborah saw that Barak was not up to the task. Her willingness to go to war was a mark of her faith in the Lord. She didn't have a thirst for blood and she wasn't trying to prove how tough she was or how qualified she was as a warrior. She recognized that the Lord selling their foe, Sisera, into the hand of a woman was backward from the very beginning. Deborah and Jael didn't kick tail because they were as strong as men or as brave as men or the same as men. The victory did not mark the disestablishment of exclusively male combatants. These women, rather, pointed clearly to the Lord's unsearchable knowledge and wealth of power— that He could use such unfit candidates[8] to accomplish such might. They were the exception, not the rule.

In the unfortunate face of male abdication, God used a backward approach to get the job done. This is how the Lord often operates. "For the foolishness of God is wiser than men, and the weakness of God is stronger than men" (1 Corinthians 1:25). If Deborah is a biblical argument for

---

[7] Whenever Israel is counted or armies are mustered, it is men who are counted. Numbers 1 is an example.

[8] In Jeremiah 50:37; 51:30; Nahum 3:13; and Isaiah 19:16, God describes failing and ineffective troops as women.

women in combat, the Book of Judges would also fill militaries with physically unqualified people like Ehud, pencil-necks like Gideon, degenerates like Jephthah, and bullies like Samson—not exactly the noble lineup we like to see in our nation's heroes. Deborah's victory was not hers. Neither was it a victory for womankind, feminism, or egalitarianism. The victory was the Lord's, who is so mighty He can use weak vessels to His great glory.

Who Washes the Dishes
After Feminism?

To comment on the stupidly named "Mommy Wars" is a poor expenditure of energy. All that can be said with certainty on the topic of women in the workforce is that real life is far more complicated than ideal-driven bickering. Most women for most of history have not had a choice in the matter, whether that meant they worked publicly or didn't. For those who live when and where there is such a thing as choice about working, there are still many women who do not have the choice and who are not free to choose enjoyable work that they are good at. Of the small percentage able to choose whether to work *and* which work to do, some are correct in their belief that the work they choose has some lofty worth, and some are not. Some are correct in believing they are good at that work, and some are not. Ideals have little to do with any of it.

But we are being silly if we imagine that *we* discovered these problems. In 1869, John Stuart Mill, that political philosopher from some history class, went to Parliament and made a big speech about how lousy it was for women to be treated differently than men by custom and law. His 1869 essay "The Subjection of Women" argued for women's property and inheritance rights and was a radically forward-thinking treatment of the topic of women in society.

Here's where this protofeminist came down on the Mommy Wars:

> If, in addition to the physical suffering of
> bearing children, and the whole responsibility
> of their care and education in early years, the
> wife undertakes the careful and economi-
> cal application of the husband's earnings to
> the general comfort of the family; she takes
> not only her fair share, but usually the larg-
> er share, of the bodily and mental exertion
> required by their joint existence.

(Let's translate for easiness: Having babies and taking care of them is, like, crazy hard on the mom. Then she pretty much always ends up doing most of the heavy lifting in terms of housework.)

> If she undertakes any additional portion, it
> seldom relieves her from this, but only pre-
> vents her from performing it properly.

(If she has something else to do on top of all the house stuff, it doesn't make the house stuff any easier, and she has even less time to do it how she wants it done.)

> The care which she is herself disabled from
> taking of the children and the household,
> nobody else takes; those of the children who
> do not die, grow up as they best can, and the
> management of the household is likely to be
> so bad, as even in point of economy to be a
> great drawback from the value of the wife's
> earnings.

(Get real. Nobody else is going to do the housework just because Mom is gone all day. The kids can't get as much of her attention if she isn't there to give it to them. Whatever money she earns will have to go toward trying to make up the difference.)

> In an otherwise just state of things, it is not,
> therefore, I think, a desirable custom, that
> the wife should contribute by her labour to
> the income of the family. In an unjust state
> of things, her doing so may be useful to her,
> by making her of more value in the eyes of
> the man who is legally her master; but, on
> the other hand, it enables him still farther
> to abuse his power, by forcing her to work,
> and leaving the support of the family to her
> exertions, while he spends most of his time in
> drinking and idleness.

(So Mom going out to make money is not really going to make things easier on her. Dad might appreciate it some, but he isn't going to pick up so much of the housework that she won't still end up doing a lot more, in addition to her outside work. *It's possible he would even spend that extra money on beer and football-related stuff.*)

We don't need this irreverent paraphrase when there's actual research to suggest J. S. M. was on to something; see, for example, *Fast Forward Family*, edited by Elinor Ochs and Tamar Kremer-Sadlik. Or maybe there's enough anecdotal evidence in your own head to save you the trouble of reading about it. This state of affairs has led to lots of bragging about husbands who do all the cooking (the ideal husband is, apparently, the help). The Food Network and HGTV have done their parts by making cooking and home-gussying into glamorous status symbols. But so far, there's no House Cleaning Channel making it really cool to scrape fossilized farina from the underside of an aquarium. Household aesthetic pursuits notwithstanding, informal polls suggest that there are still a lot of husbands whose domestic performance only *rhymes* with "bragworthy."[9] For all the advances we've supposedly made, a lot of human females still don't feel like things are fair at all. Another job the wife always ends up having to do is tallying His Funtime vs. Mine. This can get rough on the torrid love affair the contemporary marriage is required to be.

So, what to do? Well, there's always complaining, and thinking the government should or could fix this somehow. There's remembering that when there's a man on the scene, he's probably the one cleaning the gutters, chasing jackals out of the attic, and doing other yucky stuff that is self-evidently Not Mom's Job, and maybe all that should count for something. And there's also acknowledging that facts are true, and that housekeeping is a fact of life. Girls, in the aggregate, are the ones making the food, washing the dishes, putting the dishes away, figuring out what food to make next, making the food, and so on. Even in households where the in-house tasks are more evenly distributed, wives are almost certainly the ones managing everyone's clothes, keeping track of everyone's schedule, knowing about things like cleaning blinds and pantries, and not being able to

---

[9] "Nagworthy."

catch up on Candy Crush this evening.

Finally, there is the intriguing data put forth by the U.S. Department of Labor about what women do when they don't stay home. Of the top twenty jobs held by women in this liberated nation in 2012, all but a few can be categorized as childcare or education, food service, housekeeping, nursing or personal care, and secretaries or clerical work.[10] Kids, food, cleaning, sick people, and balancing the books . . . seems like I've heard of a job like this. Most women who cash in on the chance to work go into what used to be called "women's work." These things can be done voluntarily for one's loved ones or on a mercenary basis for strangers while we pay strangers to do them for us. Our choice!

---

[10] The remaining few are positions in sales or lower-level management; http://www. dol.gov/wb/stats/20LeadOcc_2012_txt.html (accessed 12/10/2014).

Peace and/or Quiet

In the Grimm Brothers' fairy tale "The Fisherman and His Wife," a man catches a fish that offers him a wish in return for being released. The thoughtful fisherman goes back to his hovel and asks his wife what she would like, and she requests a nice cottage. The fish grants the wish, but the wife is not satisfied. When the man returns, she sends him back to ask for an even bigger house. The fish obliges, but the wife wants more. She keeps sending the fisherman back, demanding that she be made king, then emperor, and then pope. Finally, she tells the man to have the fish make her like God. The fish sends the man back home, where he finds his wife sitting in their original hovel.

The point? Women have never been voiceless or powerless; in fact, their power is their voice. It is not the broad voice of journalism or the mighty voice of government, but the unavoidable one at the beginning and end of every day. Physicists and men agree that power is work over time. Hassle a guy about something long enough and, like the parabolic judge, he will probably do what is being endlessly asked of him, just to get some quiet.

Complicating a man's desire for quiet, however, is his competing desire for personal access to a woman. This desire moves men to conform to social conventions governing male-female relationships and to make some effort at practices considered normal. They commit exclusively to one female for the duration of a relationship, compile thoughtful playlists, and put down the lid in shared water closets.

However, men do not often think about practices or abstractions that belong primarily in the world of women. They do not generally care about mean girls; weddings; uneven bars or the balance beam; the circumstances under which babies are born; the ease of purchasing nail polish, organic grapeseed oil, or Appletinis; Pinterest; or anything relating to children other than their own. They are barely aware of things women think about constantly. Left alone, no man would begin to form an opinion on these or similar topics.

But due to their desire for personal access to a woman, men are not left alone. The woman to whom a man has access cares about certain things, and she wants him to care about at least some of them too. The things she thinks about constantly are, by definition, important to her. If they are important, they must be important to everyone, and he is important to her, and all her important things must hang together.

This is not a reciprocal situation. The only thing a man wants a woman to care about are the details of his own comfort in which she is directly involved. The man has to figure out that the woman wants him to care about her care-things. Then he has to figure out that to a woman, caring means agreeing. So the man comes to care about the woman's care-things in his own way. He agrees with what she thinks, in the sense that he maintains the peace by appearing to do so. His mother cleaned up with Ajax, so he keeps Ajax under his sink until he meets a petite girl with wavy hair and a spray can of Lysol. *A man's personal view on any primarily female topic is nearly always the view of the woman to whom he has access.* If he had access to a different woman who took the opposite view, he would claim that opposite view as his own.

This is how the world became a place where the goofiest of experiments have become impermissible to point out as such. The changes wrought by feminism would not have taken place without the acquiescence of the men who were infamously running things. The first guy to put a *Widen Bra Straps Now* pin on his coat is the husband of a woman who wants a world with wider bra straps. Let it never be said that the women of the prefeminist era were powerless. It is certain that, *left alone*, men would not have opened the franchise, the military, public office, or the pulpit to women. Neither would men have given such notions any serious attention if they were proposed without serious intent. But no intent is more serious than that of a woman with a righteous cause.

The work of feminism was to make its unhinged ideas about fairness into care-things for a lot of women. It didn't take much force to go that distance. Convincing people that they are being mistreated rivals the success rate of brownies. Feminists took the darkest thoughts of a chronically misused woman on a bad day and made them the default perspective of the female population as a whole. The occasional experiences of feeling unappreciated, overdrawn, excluded, and patronized were recast as intolerable and malicious norms. Providing a woman with a house, carpeting, *and* a vacuum cleaner became a crime for which a man should be punished, both publicly and privately. It became forbidden to suggest that a category of people that pretty much can't do chin-ups is not the best pool from which to recruit wranglers of thuggish criminals. Noticing that one kind of NBA has no trouble remaining independently solvent and the other does is allowable only as evidence that more feminism is needed. As a pragmatic system, feminism is hard to argue with.

It's just as well—because arguing with feminism isn't allowed anyway. To care is to agree. A few calculating men give the appearance of embracing feminist ideals to gain access to more sexually available women. But most do for the same reason they yield to any idea of female origin: to end the badgering, or more charitably, to make the women they love happy. Badgers, though, are hardy folk, and mistreatment is the charge that never runs out. So men keep trying to care by pretending to agree with things. Votes for women! #HeForShe! Step in time!

On a small scale, male quietism succeeds in producing moments of longed-for quiet. But the grace of quietness is actually given to women: "Let your adorning be the hidden person of the heart with the imperishable beauty of a gentle and quiet spirit, which in God's sight is very precious" (1 Peter 3:4). The strength of Deborah, Esther, and Catherine of Siena is not that they weren't afraid to speak up. Their stories show that making a habit of being quiet means a woman's voice will go a long way when things get colossally messed up every thousand years or so. Feminism's constant drip of complaints and accusations has only made men downright foolhardy in their practice of going along to get along. *You don't want me to open the door for you? Well, okay. You think it's only fair if, instead of running our house, you leave it every morning so you can be run by somebody else like I am? Mmmkay. Girls deactivating IEDs? Yup. Go for it.*

So now in our country, we are mad that women make less money over a lifetime because they voluntarily work less over a lifetime. We suit up our daughters in helmets and boots and hope the men they've gone to fight don't do what soldiers have always done to women. We use terms like "unplanned pregnancy," as if the cause of pregnancy were both unknown and unavoidable. An illiterate peasant from any century before the twentieth would laugh at us until her belly hurt, but it's hard to know whom she'd really be laughing at: the women who fabulized these notions or the men who went along with them.[11]

A considerate man is aware that things are different for women than they are for him. He is sympathetic toward the woman to whom he has access, and he is likely to do kind things for her, like letting her use the wish he received from a magical fish. But men give themselves away by never being jealous of women, and this is what feminism really finds unacceptable. In the feminist way of thought, it is not enough for women to have everything men have. It is also necessary that every hardship unique to women either be eliminated or suffered by men. Feminism has succeeded in getting women to be kings and emperors, and it's working on the pope thing. But the abolition or de-sexing

---

[11] *False dichotomy.*

of all female pain will require that some alterations of the human experience be made at the divine level. Feminists are already making every effort to get this done (Step 1 is a religious conversion to science). It's this kind of insanity, dreamed up by insatiable women and enabled by lazy men, that will eventually have us all back in grubby fish-hovels.

If this seems far-fetched, it is only because we are so accustomed to hearing new demands that we have become immune to their outlandishness. *The woman whom you gave to be with me, she gave me the fruit of the tree, and I caved.* Even the progressive age of feminism has failed to offer humanity anything new.

Put Your Name on It

To put a name on something is to ascribe value. A name on the labels of jackets, gym shoes, and lunch boxes ensures safekeeping of those items. When a library's name is stamped on the inside of a book cover, it sends a message to the patrons. A grocery store puts its brand on products when they judge the quality to be worthy of their name. Marking with a name shows pride and responsibility.

When George Clooney's wife took his last name, feminists fumed. She did the world a disservice, they claimed. Her act demonstrated that women aren't as important as men. She compromised her own identity by taking the name of her husband. The criticisms went on and on. Their reaction was a very "half-empty" handling of the situation. Then again, this comes as no surprise. Defenders of women are ever ready to throw another woman under the bus if she isn't riding the right bus the right way. Feminists dedicate themselves to the right treatment of women but often fail to consider kindness and support and encouragement as relevant to the cause.

They are especially critical in the Clooney case because a famous woman has failed to uphold their rigid orthodoxy. Mrs. Clooney let them down. As the feminists see it, she should have known better about her rights as a woman (she's a *lawyer*, for goodness's sake!). What this outpouring of dissatisfaction thoroughly missed is that to "take" something from another person (in this case, a name) is simply receiving a gift from that person.

A half-full view of the situation would have recognized that Mr. Clooney considers his bride to be valuable. Things become speculative at this point with regard to the Clooneys in particular, but it is at least reasonable to say in general that a man offers his name to a woman as a sign that he treasures her. He is concerned with her preservation and safekeeping. He does not want to lose her. She is his to have and to hold, and the name cements that vow. He is also hers, and he is proud to say it, and anyone who gives her trouble will have him to deal with.

Feminists determined that wearing a name indicates inferiority and cheapens value because that is how feminism operates. It sees no good in a name offered out of love. We could ask the feminists how it would be better for Mrs. Clooney to keep her father's name rather than her husband's, but we would never be that mean. We can keep things straightforward, reasonable, and much more pleasant just to see a name as a particularly heartfelt wedding gift from a loving husband. He values his bride so much that he is willing to put his name on her. He will not hide the fact that she is his, no matter what she says or does. She may never finish her master's degree or clean the bathtub properly. She may lose every *Who Wore It Best?* lineup. She may chase the Schwan's man off her lawn with a Garden Weasel. All of that and everything else will be done or undone in his name. Think of it! The guys are really taking quite a risk. A lady writes a series of crazy letters to the editor about the status of dog poop at the city park, and her husband's name ends up in the paper every time. "Was that your wife who . . . ?" Yes. Yes, it was.

What's in a name, then? A lot! It's that group of letters which holds us close to those most dear. This is important with respect to our identity in the Church too. In Baptism, Christ puts His name on us and there is great rejoicing. He pledges to care for us throughout our lives and He makes good on that promise, even when we embarrass Him, fail Him, and cause Him shame. Still, His name is on us and we are His. This is all recorded in the Book of Life. We are heirs with Him and our name seals that truth. Forgiveness of sins, life, and salvation are ours because we are Christians, which is to say, we are Christ's. To wear His name is precisely what makes us valuable and important.

Christ does not force His name on anyone. The blessings of Baptism may be rejected by anyone who no longer wishes to be called a Christian. Similarly, anyone can decline the gift of a name from a loving parent or spouse. But Christians, the Clooneys, and a world of families who like liking one another have found that a name is a really special thing to share with people we love.

THE FAMILY OF GOD

Church is all fine and good for the fine and good. The perfect families of DadMomKidKid, the happy newly-weds, the grandma whose dear ones take up three pews when they're in town for her birthday, the elders and their respectable wives—they belong here.

And then there's everybody else. There's the woman with kids but no husband (and another one over there, and another one in the back). That couple who . . . well, shouldn't they have a baby by now? The people who fill a whole row with children who don't have the same last name. The lady who brings her grandkids every week because their parents won't. That girl who must have something wrong with her if she still isn't married. Those poor people who lost their son. The woman whose husband is home with the TV and their kids because he doesn't want them getting brainwashed at church. The couple whose adult children sleep in every Sunday, even though they were in church and Sunday School every week growing up.

Well, nobody's perfect. At least those people are still coming, right? If church is for forgiveness, it doesn't do any good for a bunch of people who have done everything right to be the only ones here. Then again, these people we've just looked at—the ones whose lives look right, *and* the ones for whom things haven't gone according to plan—they aren't the only ones here.

There's King David and Michal, his wife who never had a baby. Oh, and Bathsheba, the wife he stole from a guy he had killed. And Abigail, also another guy's wife. And his other wives, Ahinoam, Maacah, Haggith, Abital, and Eglah. That's quite a family.

There's Abraham, with Sarah and Isaac. Hagar and Ishmael . . . they don't come anymore.

There's Martha, probably thinking about the roast she's got in the oven instead of the Word of God we're all supposed to be listening to. And Mary. I wonder if she made the bed this morning. And Lazarus. Kind of a weird setup those three have got.

There's Rahab the hooker, and ever-so-great-grandmother of Jesus.

There are Isaac and Rebekah with one of their twins. Did you know the other one became such an enemy of God that there's a whole book of the Bible written against his descendants?

Look at all of Jacob's kids and their moms. Yikes, their house must be a tricky place to live.

There's Esther, queen bee of a pagan king's harem, and rescuer of her people. I still don't get why her uncle Mordecai put her up for that whole thing, but I guess it worked out.

There's Adam with Eve, the mother of all the living, and the person who dragged our whole race down into sin.

There's blessed Mary. That lady has had so much crazy stuff said about her it's hard to know what to believe. And St. John with her. It's so sweet how he takes care of her.

There are Lois and Eunice with Pastor Timothy. I don't think I've ever even seen his dad.

There's that Samaritan lady who . . . well, best construction. She's here, that's what matters.

That's what matters. The family of God has as many awkward Christmases, sad estrangements, stupid feuds, barren wombs, heartbreaking losses, steps and halfs and seconds and thirds as our own families. That's not to say that it doesn't matter. Broken families are not God's intent for His people; they are an evil caricature of all that is good and holy (Malachi 2:14–16). This is why it is so important for us to remember that He is our true Father. The men and women to whom we are born are sinners; our brothers and sisters hurt and disappoint us; husbands and wives use their intimacy to maim rather than to comfort; our children resent and embarrass us; we all fail the people we should love most. But our Father calls us to repent so that we can be together at the house of our true mother, the Church; to gather around her table at peace with one another (Matthew 5:23–24).

The Honoré de Balzac novel *Le Père Goriot* tells the story of a father undone by his own adoration of his daughters. Driven to his deathbed by their shameless exploitation of his love, Father Goriot cries, "There is a God! Ah! Yes, yes, there is a God, and He has made a better world for us, or this world of ours would be a nightmare." How well so many people know this. When families come apart or never come together, the guilt, shame, or regret (misplaced or not) can be a crushing weight. There is no remedy on earth for relationships that go wrong and everything that comes of that.

But the family of God is bigger than our families, our congregations, and even our time. When we gather in His house and in His name, it is "with angels and archangels and all the company of heaven" (from the Proper Preface of the liturgy). The altar of God is open to His children of all time and space. The record shows that the family of God has never been as beautiful as we'd like, but at the head of the Table is the Father of us all. Father Goriot understands: "The whole world turns on fatherly love; fatherly love is the foundation of society; it will crumble into ruin when children do not love their fathers." Our Father is the only hope we have of getting this family in order.

Here on earth, our divine family does not have a bunch of perfect portraits on the mantle and uncomplicated return address labels for the Christmas cards. What we have in common is our repentance of the sin that is our birthright. We pray together for our prodigals to return, and that we would all get better at loving one another than we are at loving our grudges. Loving and getting along with the brothers and sisters with whom we are united in repentance is really loving our Father. He *has* made a better world for us. When that reunion comes, we will find ourselves members of a family that is whole and happy forever.

To the Virgins, to Make Much of What They Are

To speak of virginity as a gift seems strange. We think of virginity as an omission, so how can it be a gift? But human biology naturally moves most people toward the relinquishment of virginity;[12] therefore, choosing to retain it is an essentially unnatural act. Here is one of many ways that God teaches us that *natural* is unequal to *good*. A tornado is as natural as a sunny spring day; a mother rabbit eats her babies as naturally as another mother swaddles hers. Nature is fallen, so the natural impulses people experience are untrustworthy. Living by our feelings or desires makes us slaves to appetites ruined by sin.

Choosing to remain virgin past the age of physical maturity is an act of trust. It is believing that indiscriminate acting on one's sexual hankerings is inhumane. An animal in heat is the famous metaphor for a sexually undisciplined person. Then again, if a goose or a wolf has the good sense to refrain from hooking up with a stranger, we malign the animal population by associating it with the mindless sexual intercourse many humans would like to see regularized.

---

[12] There are some people who have no desire to engage in sexual intimacy. There is nothing wrong with them; "It is good for them to remain single" (1 Corinthians 7:8), and that is all that needs to be said on the topic.

The virgin is someone who is able to see that impulsive copulation degrades both people involved.

The virgin also believes that God's establishment of marriage is worthy, and that whatever it is one may be missing out on, it cannot be gained by arrogation. A sexual experience or relationship is neither substitute nor practice for the holy, lifelong bond between man and wife. Extramarital intercourse is to marital love as stealing from the cash register is to running the business. One can come by money either way, but only the business owner may become rich in character and legacy by virtue of noble work. The character of the habitual thief can only decay.

Guarding one's virginity is, finally, an act of wisdom. Women have more to lose by promiscuity. Their bodies are more vulnerable to disease. They pay an immeasurable price for bringing a child into the world without a committed father (though not as high a price as the child does). Stakes as high as these are foolishly left to any failure rate greater than zero percent. But society and science labor tirelessly to overpower these facts. The human animal wants cupcakes, oversleeping, and sex, all without consequences. Oversleeping seems least likely to succeed since it is still quaintly frowned upon by employers. An excess of cupcakes is also more penalized than sexual laxity. Sex, like cupcakes, does make most ladies fat, if one's body is not caused to conceal historical truths. But a baby can be removed from a rounding belly with more ease than last month's cupcakes, while antimicrobials suffice for less fattening but equally undesirable organisms. In the occasional cases in which only the *appearance* of virginity is desirable, it is usually attainable.

So those who wish to preserve their virginity in truth have little support from a culture that scorns it. But they do have some advantages. First is the blessing of God in His Word and Church, where virgins have always been honored as an exceptional class of people. The virgin "bears witness to the absolute value of the soul."[13] God and His Church value the person herself because she is made in God's image and her life shows forth His power and love. The world asks a person, "What makes your life worth living?" The Lord tells her that He has made her life, which is why it is worth living. To the world, the virgin is a waste of sexual potential and a drain on resources. The world's evaluation of coitus as pure hedonism hardly allows the act to bear any existential merit capable of being wasted. Moreover, God made resources so that virgins could use them along with everyone else. He did not earmark nectarines, nitrogen, fossil fuels, and snails for the "sexually active." The life of every virgin confesses the inherent worth of humanity, the pinnacle of creation, the proof and object of God's love.

The virgin's second advantage is that the matter remains fundamentally private. Even the nosiest roommate is owed nothing beyond "That's none of your business." The virgin may speak of her station if she wishes, but she is under no obligation. Her reputation is entrusted to Christian minds, all of which are called to active charity. Should she be slandered, she stands in the blessed company of the mother of Jesus.

The third advantage the virgin has is the comfort of a

[13] Gertrud von le Fort. *The Eternal Woman* Trans. Marie Cecilia Buehrle. Copyright © 2010 Ignatius Press. Used by permission of Ignatius Press. All rights reserved.

clear conscience. No depth of curiosity is worth one's integrity. Innocence is an irreplaceable gift, as anyone who has forfeited theirs in any aspect of life can testify. Mystery is surely an aggravator. It is only out-chafed by guilt.

Sexual desire does not refer only to libido. A woman's desire for exclusive companionship with a man is sexual, even if her desire is not particularly for sexual intimacy. The desire for children is also sexual; that is, it is inextricable from one's sexuality as a man or a woman. There is no shame in wanting these things, and many women have found them to be their strongest motivations for marriage. It is better to marry than to burn for any of the good gifts of marriage, not just the one deified by every billboard and blockbuster. If ever anything were worth the wait, it is a marriage as free of guilt or regret as we sinners can hope to have.

But whether or not one hopes to trade the blessing of virginity for the blessing of marriage, virginity remains a holy gift. It is valuable in itself, not only because it may be made a gift to another. Seeing virginity primarily as a bit of capital toward making a godly marriage is an anemic view of chastity. Marriage is a picture of the promise God has given us that one day, we will be united forever with the true Bridegroom, our Lord Jesus Christ. Being married helps us understand what God's ultimate intent for us is, but marriage is not the real thing. Those individuals who live with the promise alone rather than relying on the image are richer for it. They are riding the bike, while married people take a slower, safer, less dignified way down the trail on training wheels. Virginity also safeguards against the vast and vile landscape of sexual sin. The problems associated with remaining virgin are, on the whole, a lot less ugly and complicated than those associated with sexual intercourse.

Again, the virgin can only believe all this, which is why deliberate virginity is necessarily characterized by trust and wisdom. For the Christian, there are hardly two nobler things. A person given over to them cannot help but grow in the right direction. The virgin structures her life around having learned good from good rather than from evil. Her habits all flow from this *habitus* of virtue.

Virginity does not benefit from being romanticized. The virgin is likely a lonely person who feels isolated from greater humanity and excluded from certain understandings. She is tactlessly infantilized even by those who should know better on the basis of courtesy, if not their shared understanding of Christian chastity. But Scripture admonishes us in words originally addressed to Pastor Timothy, "Let no one despise you for your youth, but set an example for the believers in speech, in conduct, in love, in faith, in purity" (1 Timothy 4:12). The virgin, young or old, embodies as no one else can the beauty of pristine youth *and* the wisdom of age (not to mention the ages). The maiden aunt is blessedly younger than yesterday's blushing bride. The maiden in bloom keeps conscientious vigil over ancient mysteries the worn-out matron easily forgets. For this example, all believers owe a debt of respect.

HERE COMES THE BRIDE

Ever wonder why Scripture talks about the Church as the Bride of Christ, and not the wife? Practical-minded grandmas shake their heads at girls whose heads are so full of the wedding details that they haven't thought at all about the remainder of their lives. A boring old marriage will be all that's left to show for that big, silly blowout. Brides are good for a day, but if a lady is going to drag a wedding into her personal history, real life is about being a wife.

Yet when God talks about His beloved people, He often sounds like a divine wedding planner. In Ezekiel 16 and Isaiah 61, He dresses His bride; Psalm 45 and the entire Book of Song of Solomon describe a royal wedding; Jesus describes Himself as a Bridegroom in John 3 and Matthew 22 and 25; and Scripture culminates with "the holy city, new Jerusalem, coming down out of heaven from God, prepared as a bride adorned for her husband" (Revelation 21:2).

The grandmas are right that *being* a wife is a big deal, but we learn from God's Word that *becoming* a wife is not just another day. If we can see past the farce that is the contemporary wedding, the reason is clear. In an ideal situation, the day a woman is a bride is like no other day in her life. Her wedding day is when she moves from one holy estate to another. It is the one day she may even be, with God's blessing, both a virgin and a mother.

Our time has done away with this. White dresses, trains, and veils are no longer marks of honorable purity, but pretty costumes for the person dressing up in the morning to play the part of bride. At the other end of the day, nearly everyone agrees that becoming a mother on one's honeymoon is inadvisable, though the act that causes one to become a mother is mandatory. Even Christians who frown upon acting married before marriage see nothing commendable in a bride and groom who welcome the gifts of married love as eagerly as they watched items getting marked "purchased" on their online registry. So the bride's day is denatured and demystified both morning and night. All that remains is the party in the middle, which is left with nothing to celebrate but pageantry itself. No wonder marriages don't last.

If sins of culture don't accomplish this for a woman, just plain sin and its consequences might. Countless maidens have been robbed of their virginity, and countless matrons have wailed in anguish over a womb that remains empty. Sometimes we have to fake our way through everything that's gone wrong so something that looks sort of right can come out of it. Sometimes we do everything as right as sinners can, and still have it end up wrong.

That is why our God insists upon a mystery that can give rise to so many feelings of sadness and regret. He tells us that the mystery of the two becoming one flesh is an icon, a picture, of Christ and His holy Bride, the Church. God is not rubbing our noses in all that has gone wrong in our lives. He is also not trying to embarrass us with another set of rules that make us look even more like weirdos to the unbelievers around us. He wants everything to be right for us. He wants each of us to look forward to a day of moving from one holy estate to another free of shame, with nothing secreted or suppressed. He wants His Bride to be truly beautiful, and true beauty is borne of holiness.

For us sinners, holiness can only mean one thing: forgiveness. Even a woman whose life looks right on the outside has fallen short of the perfection of loveliness the Bridegroom would have her be. Her words, motives, and desires are sinful. But "as the bridegroom rejoices over the bride, so shall your God rejoice over you" (Isaiah 62:5). I knew a man once who, well into his sixties, always referred to his wife as "my bride." An abundance of cruel comments would surely suggest themselves to an uncharitable person who looked at this lady for evidence of brideliness. Outside of her radiant smile and joyful heart, there wasn't much of that left. To her husband, though, that one day of mystery defined her. She had become his, and that was her beauty. He saw the *truth* in what his bride had been and what she had become for him; the *goodness* of their faithful commitment; the *holiness* of the God who had given them to each other. Since she had been his bride one day, she would be his bride as long as they both would live. This is the miracle that characterizes the people of God. He has made us His, and therefore He sees us as He made us, world without end.

The bride exists in a day. She epitomizes the timeless connection between past and future that we call the present, and this makes her the most eternal creature time has to show for itself. This is part of why the Church is the Bride. As time's closest approximation of eternity, she is time-bound humanity's best match for the One who was and is and is to come. For some blessed people, the promise of the heavenly consummation means an even more wondrous, beautiful, rapturous love than the one they knew in this life. For many others, knowing that Christ came from heaven to seek His holy Bride means that the nuptial do-over we wish we could have is real. Everything that was wrong will be gone. The day when the redeemed of God move from glory to glory cannot get ruined or have an asterisk. The Bridegroom will "present you holy and blameless and above reproach" (Colossians 1:22), unashamed because He bore all shame, unafraid because His Word is truth. Come quickly, Lord Jesus.

MARRIAGE: NOT ACTUALLY THE MOST CHRISTIANEST THING EVER

Christians are known as the family of God, and for good reason. God is our Father, the Church is our mother, and Jesus is our Brother according to the flesh. All Christians are adopted into this family through Baptism, and we commonly refer to one another as brothers and sisters in Christ. We speak this way because it is true, but the truth is famous for hurting. There is no more coveted demographic in the Church than the "young family," that archetypal model of happiness consisting of a dad, a mom, and some appropriate number of clean children. It's a short step from admiring beautiful families to making everyone else feel second-rate. A person who is alone in the world is likely to feel left out of the *family* of God. But God Himself is explicit on the point that to be alone in the world is a distinct blessing, albeit a costly one.

When we speak of celibacy, we do not necessarily mean virginity. Celibacy refers to sexual abstinence. Virgins are obviously celibate, but other Christians are also called to celibacy. Widows are celibate, as are people who have been divorced. The married may have times of celibacy due to illness or separation. First Corinthians 7 also teaches that a married couple may practice limited abstinence for the purpose of prayer, but that they should not do so extensively. But this same passage of Scripture extols a life of celibacy as a higher gift than marriage, and there are several reasons why.

Celibacy benefits a person spiritually, as St. Paul explains:

> I want you to be free from anxieties. The unmarried man is anxious about the things of the Lord, how to please the Lord. But the married man is anxious about worldly things, how to please his wife, and his interests are divided. And the unmarried or betrothed woman is anxious about the things of the Lord, how to be holy in body and spirit. But the married woman is anxious about worldly things, how to please her husband. (1 Corinthians 7:32–34)

A spouse is one of the greatest gifts God gives, but married people can testify that having one is at least as much work as a puppy or a boat. Being unmarried means a lot more available mental energy, which Scripture designates for holiness and "things of the Lord." Celibacy also reduces one's potential for a sinfully wrathful reaction to a pair of socks left on the stairs. Having two sinners in close quarters certainly heightens the complexity of their total sin, even if the absolute occurrence were to remain the same. Hence the sensitive advice, "Those who marry will have worldly troubles, and I would spare you that" (1 Corinthians 7:28).

Second, the celibate person stands against the romantic view that a person's worth is measured by the emotional weight of her human relationships. This standard is clearly slanted in favor of the happily married. But Jesus died for the celibate person as much as He did for the beloved spouse (not to mention the unbeloved spouse). "Precious in the sight of the LORD is the death of His saints" (Psalm 116:15), no matter how many people show up for a particular saint's funeral. Every person ever born is a testimony to the love and power of the Creator, and His love for any one of us is greater than the love all of humanity combined could offer. The Christian Church is the one place human life is not a popularity contest or a successibition. We are all sinners before God, and we are all redeemed by His love, and that is what each of us is worth.

Third, celibate Christians are a treasure for the Church. They are able to give more of themselves to the people of God because they are not called upon to give most of themselves to a spouse. This freedom even becomes a gift to the world, which often finds the celibate person more liberal with time and resources than a married person. A greater sacrifice of service is not the purpose of a celibate person's life, but it is a benefit.

But to speak of reasons alone is to give too much attention to *reason*, and not enough to *alone*. At this point, we would do well to hear from a celibate person. Father Larry Janowski, a poet and Franciscan priest, speaks of his acceptance of the celibate life in this way:

> If this is what
> it costs to hold
> at heart a hollow
> where no sparrow

lives (nothing alive

that needs light),

if this is what God

expects from Yes,

then it is too much

today, although

I pay it anyway . . .

(from "What Celibacy Is")[14]

Another gift of the celibate person to the Church is her forbearance toward those whom the Lord in His wisdom set in families. Even the memory of loneliness, which some married people may have, is no approximation of the daily experience of going home to no one, of being uniquely tied to no heart on earth. No act of gracious hospitality or invitation to share in familial society is the sparrow for the heart established in earthly hollowness. The battle for this heart is that it be set on things above, rather than emptied of hope by its lifelong trial of human solitude.

Celibacy can be received with grace or displeasure, but it is never given by accident. The way Scripture speaks of celibacy shows us that it is not an oversight when God does not grant the gift of marriage. It is not, as the Germans would say, an *Unding* (an un-thing). No one is celibate because God forgot her. "We do not choose gifts, remember?" writes Elisabeth Elliot on the topic of singleness. "We are given them

---

[14] Larry Janowski, *BrotherKeeper* (Chicago: Puddin'head Press, 2007), 48.

by a divine Giver who knows the end from the beginning, and wants above all else to give us the gift of Himself."[15] Failing to recognize celibacy as a gift muddles it in a kind of pseudo-mysticism that says, "If I want to be married and I'm not, I don't have the gift of celibacy," as if celibacy were not a situation of fact. It is not a lack of calling or position. Celibacy is a positive, substantive gift and, like all true gifts, it is selected by the Giver, not the receiver.

Even for those who receive the gift of celibacy willingly, the divine observation remains: it is not good for the man to be alone. The default setting of humanity is to be united to another person. Those for whom this is not the case feel misunderstood and excluded at times, or maybe it would be better to say that at times, they feel understood and included. The family of God should lighten this cross rather than add to its weight. For those who return each evening to an empty home, every visit to the house of God is their earthly homecoming. The family of God is where every member is loved for who she is and nothing else, and she is missed when she is gone. In Christian traditions that do not formalize the celibate life, it is all the more important for celibate people to be welcomed to and included in the life of the Church. Their often unseen work deserves the thanks of everyone whose waiting spouse or crying babies of all ages excused them to leave sooner.

---

[15] Elisabeth Eliot, *Let Me Be a Woman* (Wheaton, IL: Tyndale House, 1976), 34. Copyright © 1976, 2004 by Tyndale House Publishers, Inc. Used by permission of Tyndale House Publishers, Inc. All rights reserved.

"In life no house, no home My Lord on earth might have."[16] There is no greater model for the celibate life than Jesus Himself. He and all who follow this particular path are a reminder to the whole family of God that this world is not our true home. The God who emptied Himself for our sake will one day fill every heart eternally. The celibate person knows the other part of human life, that which the married person cannot know. But one day, we will know fully, as all of us, single or married, are now fully known by our Lord.

---

[16] "My Song Is Love Unknown" (LSB 430:6).

Earthen Vessels

A vessel is vulnerable by nature. Its intended contents determine its construction. A ten-gallon pickle crock doesn't receive the same treatment as Great-Grandma's bone china cream pitcher. The pickle crock we park in the garage until the cucumbers attempt their annual ascent to dominance; the cream pitcher is displayed in a closed china cabinet. We'd hate to have to choose between them. They are both valuable to us, though in different ways.

When vessels were earthen and potsherds cut feet, it was more clear that vessels must be guarded. One moment of careless inattention, and a valuable item could be lost forever. Nearly as quickly can a person be shattered, a life ruined. The world is full of people who don't care about breaking other people's things, or even derive a sick pleasure from doing so. We protect the breakable objects in our house from destructive forces like dogs, wind, and preschoolers. Only an inhuman lack of care would leave a vulnerable *person* at the mercy of the world's monsters. The Lord God made man from the dust of the ground, not an amalgam of chemically manipulated oils. We break.

A plastic time sees protective concern as insulting. Women claim to scorn fake, plastic Barbie but insist they are not china dolls. They refuse to admit their own vulnerability because it is born of a weakness they will not see as good. They want pickles made in cream pitchers and all of it balanced on the front porch rail in a bad part of town. Then they rage about the monsters who broke the cream pitcher, the ruined pickles, and the town that failed to make it a fine thing to leave fragile perishables absolutely anywhere. Monsters are at fault for their monstrosities. But it is criminally negligent to fail to inform a vulnerable person that monsters are real, some parts of town are best avoided, cream pitchers are lousy for pickle making, and things that are left out get broken. Ideals are of no use in a fallen world.

It is also spiteful and cruel to fail to explain to a fearfully and wonderfully made person that she is fearful and wonderful. We have a treasure in earthen vessels (2 Corinthians 4:7), and all we must do to see that God did not roll the dust of the earth into billions of identical terra-cotta pots is look around. We can also tell, with only a look, that half of us are made to hold something specific.

There is hardly a greater marvel on earth than that its weaker creatures should perform humanity's most staggering work—except, perhaps, that anyone should refuse to recognize and esteem it as such. The ghettoizing of motherhood into a few bothersome years of a woman's life is the essence of chauvinism. It belittles the work, the person at whose significant pains the work is accomplished, and the One who gave the work and called it good.

Women are the "weaker vessel" (1 Peter 3:7) because they are more vessellish. A man must pull his own weight, but a woman is made to carry the weight of another in addition to her own. She is, as a kind, more lightly built so that she is able to bear the most delicate freight of all—another person. This is not to diminish the difference between men and women to one of surface area, as there are many individual exceptions to any general rule. But woman's generally finer construction is the secondary mark of her provision to protect the fragile cargo she is equipped to carry. This work weakens her by virtue of its inherent demands. Even those who never bear in their own bodies bear the marks of that potential both in body and soul.

Woman's literal capacity is fundamental to her essence. Her ability to give life is relevant beyond any actual event of it happening. It affects and defines her entire person. Having been made to perform her greatest work of love in a certain way, she cannot help performing all works of love in a way that testifies to that. Maternity is a property of everywoman, if not every woman. She is not the weaker vessel only if she is actively carrying another, but because she could be or has been able to. Motherhood is not merely a year of attachment, a few years of need, and some decades of dependence that dissipate into a general appreciation. It is where womanly sympathy, diligence, perceptiveness, ingenuity, or sacrifice are likely to be most fully called upon in a woman's life. That a woman possesses gifts a child needs whether or not she herself has a child is a cosmic bonus.

This is not to descend into sentiment or stereotype. The actual experience of motherhood is the greatest evidence many women have of their own lack of maternal gifts, even women who truly love being mothers. Not every woman considers herself nurturing, patient, temperate, or whatever attribute is popularly thought of as maternal. They are correct in their self-assessment, since children demand more goodness from their mothers than any woman has. They have also missed the point. Being maternal is an intrinsic feminine quality. Every female possesses it in her own way, without reference to kissing of boo-boos or any other vapid proxy for motherhood. The least maternal woman—by character, childlessness, or both—is more maternal than the most arguably maternal man on earth. "Maternal" is not the title of a category under which mommy-like attributes fall. It is an attribute in itself, not of personality, but of essence and being. It is given to every woman by the Maker who made her a woman, and it is shown forth in every woman's life uniquely.

Women are obviously able to do more than bear children, which is a comfort especially to those who do not. The gift of the form is given no less to women who, for whatever reason, function otherwise. However, this does not permit devaluing the maternal function, which is the foundation of the vaunted female form. Relentless disclaiming of motherhood has come to tyrannize all discussions of woman, so that we can only regain our perspective on her if we go back to speaking of something else. A cream pitcher can be used to beautify a tableau, as an herb planter, to hold erasers or kitty litter, in a Rube Goldberg machine, or to build a ziggurat of cream pitchers to the heavens. But habitually favoring any of these alternatives ultimately calls into question the intention for and value of cream pitchers. Denigrating the function renders the form defenseless against exploitation. Preferring cream pitchers that are better for ziggurat-building results in a preponderance of cream pitchers that are bad at holding cream (to say nothing of the excess of cream pitcher ziggurats).

Valuing woman's gifts disproportionately leaves her imbalanced and dysfunctional. It is no kindness to emphasize to her constantly what *else* she is good at. This demeans what she is undeniably best at and discourages her from receiving with trust and gratitude the only earthly gift that lasts eternally. It causes her to underestimate her vulnerabilities and to undervalue her strengths. A woman is more likely to endanger herself and less likely to excel where God most intends for her to be excellent if she only hears her vessellishness spoken of as a vaguely undesirable accident of minimal consequence.

We have this treasure, born of a woman (Galatians 4:4). He spurned not the virgin's womb, taking His humanity from her body, so that what was sown in weakness will be raised in power (1 Corinthians 15:43). No matter what else we may carry, the baptized of God are always carrying in our bodies the death of Jesus (2 Corinthians 4:10). There is no shame in being vessellish, for we must contain Christ if we are to live at all. Bringing forth life through suffering is simply what Christians do, after the manner of our Lord. Those blessed to have bodies that give particular witness to this receive an honor only sinful man could fail to treasure.

To My Friend Who Has No Babies Today

Dear Lady,

Once I heard you say that God has given some women more children than you have fingers on your right hand, while He has given you none. I'm one of those women. I feel ostentatious and gaudy around you. I feel like having my babies with me is in poor taste, like I am flaunting my riches. I cringe to imagine that you might feel the same way, you who have suffered so much in your own mind and who are now subjected in real time, in public, to stare in the face the dream that hasn't come true for you. I am so sorry it hasn't. I am so sorry to think that I might be causing you more pain. I ache for the love you show my silly little people. I don't know if I could.

I sin your sins. When I see all the world's human trash with its ill-bred and empirically worthless children, I seethe to think of the pearls cast before them while your clean neck and graceful wrists and industrious fingers are bare. When another teenager turns up pregnant, I want to rage at God for what I can only see as unimaginable injustice and just plain poor planning. I want to make it right. I want to distribute the world's children sensibly by my own self-righteous fiat. I want YOU, you smart, talented, dutiful, faithful Christian person, to be a mother of nations. NOT THEM.

I see it. I didn't want to, but I love you so much I finally looked and really saw it, or saw it as well as one such as myself is able to. It was the worst thing I have ever seen. It looks like utter desolation, like horror. I can't look long. I can't believe it's the view out your window every hour of every day. Oh, you. You have lost what you never had.

But I know that we are nearsighted. I am so nearsighted outside of this metaphor that without my glasses, I can look into a dark bedroom where I know there is a digital clock and still see no light at all. This is how we see into eternity also. No eye has seen, no ear has heard, no mind has conceived what God has prepared for those who love Him. So I know that, despite its appearance to myopics like us, the desolation is not utter. I know you know too, and we walk by faith together because our sight is untrustworthy.

I cannot tell you how much I respect and admire you for not trying to take by force what God has not given. You are like the man on a lifeboat, crazy with thirst, who still knows better than to drink seawater even though his companions fall to the temptation. It must be so hard to watch them: to watch them sicken, to watch them die, to watch them live. You are the one who clings to a true hope and has the best chance of healthy survival. You trust the Lord, though He slay you.

I thank you for the witness you are to the sacred blessing of marriage, no matter what the quantifiable yield of that marriage. I thank you for the witness you are to the inherent value of femininity, no matter what the quantifiable yield of that femininity. One of the few things we probably both knew better before life taught us so much is that there is such a thing as a wife. A married lady to whom God does not give children is not an un-mother or a failed female. She is a wife. Since I'm talking to you, I will add that I happen to know you are a very good one. I wish my husband had one as good.

I don't say these things to you because I feel I don't know you well enough, or I don't know how you are doing with all this right now, or I know you are as sick of this being the relentless topic of your life as I am of the relentless topics of my life. But I want you to know that I am always thinking all these things even as you are, and I pray for you always. I'm sorry if my not saying something makes it seem like I don't care or I don't really get it. I know I don't really get it, but I try to, and I care so much.

I know you feel empty, but you bear the heaviest burden, and bearing is never without gain. God bless you, strong one.

Love,

Rebekah[17]

---

[17] A version of this letter was originally published on the blog "He Remembers the Barren," August 28, 2013 (http://herememberthebarren.com/2013/08/28/to-the-barren-ladies-i-know-and-the-ones-i-dont/).

She Respects Her Husband

L et no corrupting talk come out of your mouths, but only such as is good for building up, as fits the occasion, that it may give grace to those who hear" (Ephesians 4:29).

"Let the wife see that she respects her husband" (Ephesians 5:33).

These words are held in opposition to the unfortunately common remarks on the topic of husbandly failings.

"If I left for a week, my husband wouldn't know what to do when the toilet paper roll runs out. He never replaces it! He'd just sit there helplessly until I got back."

"My husband will literally move the trash out of his way and walk on rather than pick it up and take it outside. Come on! You're picking it up to get by! Can't you carry it ten steps more?"

"Here's what not to do: send a man to the grocery store with a list. You'll get nothing from the list but you will get a bunch of junk that you never wanted."

Such talk is corrupting. It tears down. It gives guff where there should be grace. It is disrespectful.

A wife is to be the helper, which is important work. Often, though, we'd rather run the show. To be in that position, we hack away at the credibility and capacity of the man who is rightly called to headship. So begins the standard recipe for a hostile takeover. Step 1: disqualify the leader.

Step 2: take his place. Done and done! That was easy!

This is how it will come to be said of a couple, "She definitely wears the pants." Then the pants-wearing wife will belittle her husband for his failure to wear them. She's making the problem worse. An abdicating husband may more willingly and capably wear the pants if he could just find them, but the pants are in the wrong dresser because the wife put them there.

The Christian wife, when her husband is struggling to lead, doesn't put on the pants and tell him she'll handle it all herself. Rather, she says, "Honey, I just did the laundry and your pants are right here. Hey! They look great on you! Is there anything else I can help you with?"

Rather than tearing down, a Christian wife builds up. A Christian wife takes the molehill of an empty toilet paper roll or a trash bag that needs removal or a Totino's party pizza and knows that it's totally not a big deal. These things in no way disqualify a man from headship, but if he is continually criticized for such things, he will begin to doubt his rightful role.

So Christian wives don't contribute to conversations that are loaded with criticisms and jabs. Rather, the Christian wife speaks well of her husband, both in his presence and also in the presence of others.

We are mindful of Christ's command: "Love one another as I have loved you" (John 15:12). How did He love us? "God shows His love for us in that while we were still sinners, Christ died for us" (Romans 5:8).

It's unlikely any of us will ever have to die for our spouse. We are, however, called to bear with one another and forgive one another. That requires dying to self. In this context, it especially means putting to death that prideful person inside all of us who thinks she would do the job better. As new creations, we resist the sinful urge to take a role that is not ours. We know that the proverbial pants fit the occasion of husband-hood and we build him up in this to help him grow more comfortable and confident in this God-given position.

The Fallen Ones

Give two women enough time together and they are likely to end up explaining to each other how many children they have and why. I do not mean the number that is public knowledge, but the number that is in each lady's head: the children she should or would have had, the ones she didn't have because she thought she couldn't, and the reasons behind it all. A lady with whom I have made nothing but small talk as I run errands in my little town has told me numerous times about her miscarriage decades ago. A mother of eight living children has nearly as many cemetery plots for the babies she lost before they were born. An acquaintance thought she would have one of those BIG families, but she was headed off by her disastrous labors. A stranger makes sure I understand that after twenty weeks of gestation, it is a stillbirth and not a miscarriage. Another preschool mom shows me the necklace she wears bearing the name of her baby who died unborn at thirty-eight weeks. A mentor tells me about mourning the fertility-ending surgery she felt she had to have. Someone confides to me the most heartbreaking detail of losing a tiny, tiny baby. The giving of life, each of them has learned, often means losing an awful lot of it.

How mundane is our first father's name. Adam, the "Earth Man," points us to our beginning and end. But how wondrous is our mother's, which she receives even after her unbelief and fall. Eve, "She Who Lives," points us whenever we speak of her to the essence of God's grace: that we earth-men live, impossibly, miraculously, here in time and there in eternity. To accept her utterly humble work is to receive her honor, that by her the dusty earth is filled with God's greatest work: LIFE, life in the image of God, life everlasting.

But when that gift is given so briefly, the honor twists into an unbearable weight. The wonder of a secret, hidden life bound to her own becomes a nightmare when a mother learns that she is a walking Sheol. The marvelous joy turns inside out and becomes an opaque mystery of grief. We want reasons, and there usually aren't any. The Lord, though, has a word for His people. Ecclesiastes 6, Job 3, and Psalm 58 speak of a miscarried or stillborn child, but not in the way we speak of him. We call him "miscarried," which so many mothers cannot help hearing as placing the blame particularly with themselves. But the Hebrews use the simple word *nephel*, which means "fallen." There is no special term for it, and no fault beyond that which all people bear. We are sinful from birth, sinful from conception, sinful and therefore mortal.

How very great our Lord must be to make even this right. Our comfort is to trust that He will. Martin Luther and his wife Katie lost their daughter Elizabeth when she was seven months old. In 1542, the same year another daughter, Magdalena, died in his arms, Pastor Luther wrote these words for women who had suffered a miscarriage:

> One ought not to frighten or sadden such
> mothers by harsh words because it was not

due to their carelessness or neglect. . . . These mothers should . . . have faith that God's will is always better than ours, though it may seem otherwise to us from our human point of view. . . . Because the mother is a believing Christian it is to be hoped that her heartfelt cry and deep longing to bring her child to be baptized will be accepted by God as an effective prayer. . . . Therefore one must leave such situations to God and take comfort in the thought that he surely has heard our unspoken yearning and done all things better than we could have asked.[18]

The prayer of a righteous man availeth much. The Lord is merciful to His people. It feels so much like no arms could hold our children better than our own, but the Lord's arm is mighty to save what we never could. Even now He holds every baby whose mother never got that chance.

That is all that can be said in this life; then again, sometimes the more we say, the less it helps. But there are two specific situations worthy of particular attention.

First is the problem faced by those for whom another pregnancy is a possibility. The unspeakable wrongness of being the tomb of one's child can lead us to doubt the wisdom of risking the experience again. Contemporary poet Sharon Olds gives voice to the uncertainty lingering in the minds of throngs of women in "The Unborn," in which she imagines children she could have had as lost letters or

---

[18] Luther's Works, volume 43, pages 247–50.

servants waiting to be called, and even feels a child reaching for her in the dark.

It is the job of poets to put into words what ordinary people feel but cannot articulate. Dr. Olds speaks for every lady who knows she has missed out on something. But Scripture teaches that we are Sarah's daughters if we "do not fear anything that is frightening" (1 Peter 3:6). Our God, we confess in the Nicene Creed, is the Lord and giver of life. Not even a sparrow falls without His knowing. The God who begins good works in us has promised to bring them to completion in the day of Jesus Christ (Philippians 1:6), even if not in the nine uneventful months for which we pray so fervently when a second line darkens in the test window. "Perfect love casts out fear" (1 John 4:18), and God loves us perfectly through our deepest sorrows and doubts. God lost a Son too. That same beloved Son says both "I died, and behold I am alive forevermore, and I have the keys of Death and Hades" (Revelation 1:18) and "Whoever receives one such child in My name receives Me" (Matthew 18:5).

The second situation to which we should speak is simplest when it is merely a political lightning rod. In the life of an actual woman, abortion is a soul-eating monster. We imagine that the ancient religions have died out. Marduk, Ra, Baal, Zeus, and all the rest have become curiosities for schoolkids and historians. But the cult of Molech (Leviticus 20:1–5) has had no lack of devotees from its cursed inception to the present and supposedly godless day. For those whose sorrow is exploded by true guilt and horror, our Lord pours out His heart of love and His blood for the forgiveness of sins. No altar of evil can prevail against that on which the

Lamb of God was sacrificed for the sin of the world. Jesus said of the sinful woman overcome with repentance in Luke 7 that the one who is forgiven much loves much, "And He said to the woman, 'Your faith has saved you; go in peace'" (v. 50).

WIDOWS AND THE REDEMPTION

"How lonely sits the city that was full of people! How like a widow has she become, she who was great among the nations!" (Lamentations 1:1). When Jeremiah described Jerusalem after the Babylonian captivity as a widow, he definitely understood her plight and her sad portion.

The Lord designed the good gift of marriage, establishing it as the norm for humanity throughout time. There are exceptions, of course, but those cases are just that—exceptional. In creating Eve for Adam, the Lord created marriage for humanity.

To lose one's spouse is to lose a part of one's self. Eve was fashioned from Adam's rib. There was completeness in their union from the very beginning. "Therefore a man shall leave his father and his mother and hold fast to his wife, and they shall become one flesh" (Genesis 2:24). When a widow feels that a part of her is gone, she has understood well the blessed union of marriage and the tremendous pain of its rending. In *A Grief Observed*, C. S. Lewis described this loss as an amputation.

When a woman first loses her beloved, there is an appropriate outpouring of Christian care and concern. Time goes on, though, and busy people forget the pain of a widow. Long after the funeral lunch leftovers are gone, a part of *her* is still gone. The Church may overlook the part of her that remains, hobbling as she may. There is a terrible loneliness in this.

The Church is called to care for widows. Where spontaneous compassion may fail to motivate the body of believers in this important work, the Lord still expects it and the Law still requires it. Throughout the Old Testament, God's people were repeatedly reminded to look after the sojourner, the fatherless, and the widow.[19] People in need of protection and provision occupied those categories. God instructed His faithful to be the earthly means of meeting their needs. This is how He watches over and "upholds the widow" (Psalm 146:9).

In New Testament times, the office of deacon was created as a response to the wrongful negligence of widows in the daily distribution (Acts 6:1–7). The widows needed to be fed. This was undeniably the broad work of the Church, while not specifically the narrow task of the pastors. More than just their physical needs, Scripture also urges believers to consider and call on the widows in their affliction (James 1:27). Feeding widows is good; visiting them is good too. Not every lack is strictly physical.

These biblical directives demonstrate how clearly the Lord, "protector of widows" (Psalm 68:5), understands their loneliness and is filled with compassion and love for them. While busy people might fail to see the needs of the widow and the value of her life, the Lord never would and never will. He does not count them out.

Moreover, Christ does not permit a widow to count

---

[19] Exodus 22:22; Deuteronomy 10:18; 14:29; 24:17–21; 26:12–13; Job 31:16.

herself out. The body of believers should not neglect the widow. Neither should the widow neglect her gifts and talents, purpose and value. A widow who feels she has nothing left to do, offer, or give has diminished her worth. A despairing widow may feel that her life is not worth living. A faithful widow holds fast to the promise that it is no longer she who lives, but Christ who lives in her (Galatians 2:20). This is what determines and secures her worth. He has a purpose for her.

The widow's life is ordered more directly than ever under the Lordship of Christ, her Head. As the prophet Isaiah comforted, "The reproach of your widowhood you will remember no more. For your Maker is your husband, the LORD of hosts is His name" (Isaiah 54:4b–5a). While her earthly lord's passing means that a part of her is gone, her heavenly Lord's abiding love for her is her restoration. Where her earthly lord no longer needs her help, the Lord still blesses her with occasions to serve and give and care according to her abilities and means.

The Lord used the improbable widow of Zarephath to feed His prophet Elijah in 1 Kings 17. This woman was herself in need of charity meals, and she was a highly unlikely candidate to be providing anything to anyone else. She had "nothing baked, only a handful of flour in a jar and a little oil in a jug" (v. 12). In fact, this widow's plan was to use the last of her meager resources for a final meal with her son. After that, her only plan was to die. In the absence of her husband's provision, this widow was in utter despair. She counted herself out. The Lord did not though. The Lord Himself provided for her needs, and He also gave her the ability to care for others. Through Elijah, a promise was made and kept: "The jar of flour shall not be spent, and the jug of oil shall not be empty, until the day that the LORD sends rain upon the earth" (v. 14). The Lord restored the widow to her role as helper. She who had next to nothing, she who was ready to lie down and die—she fed a prophet.

Christ does not count out the widow. Rather, He counts *on* her. Many, many years later in a temple, a widow quietly put two small coins in an offering box (Mark 12:41–44; Luke 21:1–4). Where others may have easily passed her over, our Lord not only noticed her, but He also used her to teach His disciples how extraordinary offering is not measured in terms of what a person puts in, but in terms of what a person has left when the giving is done. By giving all that she had, the supposed poor widow set her hope firmly on the Lord, and He praised her for this. While others gave out of their abundance, she offered all that she had to live on, trusting God alone to provide her with all of her needs. Ultimately, the widow demonstrated that she was only poor according to the wisdom of a foolish age. Her great wealth was secure in her priceless worth to her Lord. He restored her to her role as helper as she taught the disciples through a small, selfless act. And she wasn't the only widow in the temple with a major role to play.

Years before our Lord was teaching in the temple, He was presented there as a baby to be redeemed for the price of two birds. Anna in the temple, like the poor widow, also exemplified the standard described in 1 Timothy 5:5: "She who is truly a widow, left all alone, has set her hope on God and continues in supplications and prayers night and day." She was advanced in age, having spent only seven years with her husband and the rest as a widow. Her grief could have been a debilitating force. Anna, as all widows, had to learn to live without her other half. She dedicated her life to serving her Lord. She kept waiting and hoping for the redemption of Jerusalem (Luke 2:38). Others saw the baby Jesus coming to be redeemed at the temple. Anna knew that He actually came to be the Redeemer of all. This baby, brought by Mary and Joseph, was the one on whom she had fixed her eyes and set her hope.

The widow of Zarephath eventually understood what it meant to hope in the Lord and also knew the joy of being used by the Lord. So did the poor widow and Anna. Those dear women had felt the pain of losing a part of themselves. They understood that only the Lord could make them whole.

The faithful widow today likewise sets her hope on God and waits on Him. With time, the grief of losing her beloved may diminish. There could still be a lingering loneliness for the part of her that is gone, though. No matter what, she must not count herself out. Her Lord will not have it! Through her generosity and service, fasting and prayers, and enduring faith and hope, a godly widow has important work to do. Even if a widow is laid low and cannot carry out any remarkable functions according to our society's standards, by living her life she teaches the Church about the completion that awaits us all. She teaches us to be patient in affliction. She reminds us of that desolate city, Jerusalem, which sat like a widow. In all of this, she hopes and hopes in her Lord. She knows He will return in glory. She, along with all of God's elect, will be made whole again.

A Righteous Life

Here is a big problem: the benefits of the wisdom of age depend upon the wisdom of youth to recognize them.

In his novel *Main Street*, Sinclair Lewis puts an idea in the mind of his unheroic heroine: "She saw that Aunt Bessie did not mean to intrude; that she wanted to do things for all the Kennicotts. Thus Carol hit upon the tragedy of old age, which is not that it is less vigorous than youth, but that it is not needed by youth; that its love and prosy sageness, so important a few years ago, so gladly offered now, are rejected with laughter." This clarity of insight is unusual for the ridiculous Carol, and although she is able to see it as sad, she comes short of seeing it as wrong. But we see that wrongness easily when a beloved elder confides sadly that she has become useless. She is wrong, of course, but even if there were a case to be made on some purely pragmatic basis, she would be wrong to equate *use* with *worth*.

Scripture tells us, "But God chose what is foolish in the world to shame the wise; God chose what is weak in the world to shame the strong; God chose what is low and despised in the world, even things that are not, to bring to nothing things that are, so that no human being might boast in the presence of God" (1 Corinthians 1:27–29). The world is constantly at war with weakness. It sees every person in terms of resources, and anyone who consumes more than she contributes is a liability. For now, lingering senses of thanks and nostalgia protect those advanced in years from the world's senicidal trend, but the battle is beginning. "Quality of life" and "death with dignity" are the catchphrases of progressive thinkers. Terminally ill patients who choose to end their lives rather than become burdens to their families are rewarded with fifteen minutes of fame to advance the high-minded cause. We're all going to die, and it isn't a nice process. We'd better get that humiliating, smelly business under control.

Don't you feel sick?

Well, too bad. The Church has a job for old ladies, and if God sees fit to make a lady old, it would be cheating to try to get out of it. Scripture teaches us,

> Older women likewise are to be reverent in behavior, not slanderers or slaves to much wine. They are to teach what is good, and so train the young women to love their husbands and children, to be self-controlled, pure, working at home, kind, and submissive to their own husbands, that the word of God may not be reviled. (Titus 2:3–5)

In the surrounding verses, old men, young men, and slaves are also given instructions for how they are to live. But no one has a longer directive than the older women, and no one else's is as specific. Most interestingly, no other group of people is told that, in addition to their own good conduct, they are to act as teachers. The older women are given the particular task of teaching young women how to take care of their families. Their experience combined with their faithfulness is a gift to younger women, who often feel overwhelmed and underequipped for managing a household. A young lady needs both ideas and encouragement, and no one is more able to offer those things than someone who has already been through the trials of starting out, keeping at it, and keeping at it some more.

This brings us back to our original problem. Not all young women respond well to advice or wisdom. Some of them are too self-conscious, some are too self-confident, and some are too self-absorbed. It's hard to know who is willing to listen and who isn't. But a good teacher is someone who is available to her students. You never know who is quietly taking notes or too shy to ask a question. The first step toward being a faithful teacher is, as one is able, being easy to find. Being with family and being at church are lessons in themselves. They demonstrate the virtues of commitment and perseverance, which are two of the main things required for keeping a household running day after boring day, week after madcap week, year after vanishing year.

But the fabled wisdom of age and the older woman's responsibility to teach are not just about the good advice she has to offer. Her teaching is not merely in her long perspective on human life, but in how she lives out the years God has appointed for her. Has her time on earth made her reverent or careless? Are her words charitable or slanderous? Is she temperate, or does she follow her appetite? Does she meet hardship with grace or complaint? *Is she sticking with it after all this time?* An example of faithfulness means more to the young than they let on, and sometimes more than they can understand yet. Young people may feel unable to meet life's demands, and the middle-aged can be tempted to nihilism by its apparent futility. They need to see that when the fight is fierce and the warfare long, there are still soldiers fighting who have been at it much longer.

"Gray hair is a crown of glory; it is gained in a righteous life" (Proverbs 16:31). To be rich in years is a gift without qualification. Most humans are slow learners. When God gives long life, it is so that we have more time to grow into the understanding of Him that He would have for all His children. It is no secret that life's end usually brings with it suffering and losses of all kinds, which is why the godless would like to cut it short. But the crosses God appoints for us are always for our good. They are how we learn to rely on Him more fully and to find our comfort in His Word and prayer. We spend our whole lives claiming to be too busy to pray. If a Christian finds herself in her latter years unable to do all the things she used to, maybe longing to help like Carol's Aunt Bessie, she is still able to pray. That is a service she can offer her family, her church, and her Lord, even if she can no longer walk with a fussy baby, make supper for everyone, or change the paraments.

And what if, eventually, a Christian is unable even to pray with her whole mind? Can there really be any good in becoming an object of care? A lady who has spent her life caring for others has already answered this question. As a righteous woman gives her life's energy to those around her, she teaches that there is no more blessed work on earth than serving those whom Jesus calls "the least of these." When eventually each of us finds herself back in that category, we learn again who we are in relation to the God who saves us. He promises, "Even to your old age I am He, and to gray hairs I will carry you" (Isaiah 46:4). We are the helpless beneficiaries of His love. We were dead in our sins, and He saved us. We wither and perish, but He who never changes gives our care into the hands of people who need to learn the same lesson we once did. Our worth is not in what we do or make, but in who we are—creations of a holy God. Accepting this care with grace is a final act of trust and gratitude to Him.

Calling

"Calling" goes way back. The Lord called Adam in the garden, Abraham out from the pagans, Moses through the burning bush, and Jeremiah despite his youth. These men experienced personal revelations of God.

"But in these last days He has spoken to us by His Son" (Hebrews 1:2). The New Testament people of God are called to faith in Jesus by Holy Baptism. He gives us His voice in Holy Scripture and His proclaimed Word. That is the promise of God to this age, the age of the Church. And that means that if my landscaping spontaneously combusts while I'm having a dream about joining the circus, it doesn't mean a blessed thing.

Vocation is how Christians often talk about calling, and Martin Luther is well known for his attention to this doctrine. The error of his religious day was to think that churchy work was better than nonchurchy work. The error of our prosperous day is to think that what we like is what we are called to. If I am good at accounting, it means God wants me to have a career as an accountant. If I like photography, the studio I could add onto my house is God's will for me. My desired marital status corresponds, conveniently, to the marital status to which God is calling me! I don't like kids, which is how I knew God didn't intend for me to have any. My wants equals my calling.

It may be easiest to get to true calling through the back door, so let's start with what it isn't. Vocation is not the same as a job. For example:

> Mother is a vocation. Folding laundry is a job.
>
> Husband is a vocation. Assembling porch gliders is a job.
>
> Breadwinner is a vocation. Tinker, tailor, soldier, and spy are jobs.

We wouldn't think much of a father who spent his days waiting for a record label to recognize the genius of his ditties while his children gnawed the coffee table. Most people don't have the privilege of pursuing the job they would most enjoy or one where their gifts lie. Those who are called to the work of breadwinning must put winning sufficient bread ahead of their personal interests. We *would* think much of the songster dad if he got a job that supported his family and then used his musical talent avocationally at church. Christians do not claim a right to do what we want or like. Vocation requires us to sacrifice pride and comfort because other people often need things beneath our imagined dignity.

The beauty of vocation is not that whatever we're good at is good for us to do, but that whatever God has given us to do is good. Dr. Thomas Winger writes in his commentary on Ephesians, "The [New Testament] knows of only two callings: the call to the apostolic office, and the call to faith in Christ. . . . The Christian's calling is not normally a call to *do* something, but to *be* someone."[20] The apostolic office is not taking applications at this time, but our calling to faith in Christ through Baptism is the starting point from which we can begin to see how a Christian lives. As we look out from the font over the congregation of God's elect, and even past the church doors to the world beyond, we see that vocation directs our energy and resources to those people. We often think of vocational questions as "What does God want me to do?" A better way of putting it is "What would a Christian in my position do?"

Another way to tell a vocation from an inclination is the quit test. A married person cannot morally quit fulfilling her marital vows. A breadwinner is not free to quit providing for those whose survival requires that income. But quitting Goldman Sachs for a position at Morgan Stanley, or leaving telecommunications for a job in advertising, is no problem at all. The quit test also helps us put the matter of steward-ship in perspective. God gives us all aptitudes and loves, but our responsibilities toward family, church, and community outweigh any gift that is essentially a bonus. Sailing, poo-dle grooming, Coen brothers movies, Zumba, crochet, and community theater are all privileges, not rights. We could quit them tomorrow and everything would be fine, including our faithfulness to the God who distinguishes His creatures with all kinds of fancies in the first place. Our passions are not sacrifices of praise if they are indulged at the expense of our God-given duties.

---

[20] Thomas Winger, *Concordia Commentary: Ephesians* (St. Louis: Concordia Publishing House, 2015), 428.

So vocation is not our license to do whatever we want with our lives in Jesus' name. It cannot be a front for pursuing dreams. Vocation does not mean "what I do from eight to four thirty" or "the job, salary, and props I'll deserve after finishing this degree" or even "stewardship of my gifts." It means doing what needs to be done, which means simply that breadwinners should win bread. They should keep in mind the danger of gathering more than they need, unless they want their greed reported by a pantry packed with moldy manna. Those who are able to win bread by means of their favored talents can thank God for His benevolence. They can either take comfort or derive humility from knowing that the *way* they win bread is not a matter of vocation (if it were, leaving a job would be an abdication of one's calling). And all people can use their gifts, talents, and interests avocationally for the glory of God and the good of His people.

So much for jobs, but what about the rest of our lives? Again, the back door can be the easier way in. It is natural for a happily married person to see herself as having been called to marriage. The same cannot be said for the person whose spouse is no source of joy or the person who is involuntarily single or childless. No one whose marriage has gone south feels like sticking with it is a promising course of action. No person who pleads to God for a husband feels called to loneliness, though it is a fact of her life. No lady who knows the Two-Week Wait doubts that God is calling her to become a mother. No beloved wife feels called to widowhood, and no child who loses a parent feels called to be an orphan, though our God is the God of the fatherless and the widow. The nature of vocation is perhaps not best seen in a gift received in joy, but in a cross submitted to in trust. The selection of gifts lies with the Giver. When God's calling is not what we wanted to hear, it is no less God's calling.

God has planned good things for us. We need to remember that we see dimly (1 Corinthians 13:12), and this goes for our hearing as well. "For those who love God all things work together for good" (Romans 8:28), but we have not yet heard the whole story. The blessings God intends for us will be on His terms. This is good news for sinners. Our terms cannot help being ill-conceived. Only God is good, and the good He wills for us comes in His time and way. For this reason, the prayer of the Church is always "Come, Lord Jesus." On the day of His coming, our callings will be clear as the crystal sea of heaven. Until then, hard-of-hearing creatures are wise to claim no calling beyond the one we heard unmistakably at our Baptism, those we received at the altar of God, and those He worked irrevocably in our own bodies.

What, then, shall we say to these things? Not too much. We should never put words in God's mouth by upgrading a desire, an ideal, or a fantasy into a divine calling. We are perpetual prey to the father of lies, which means that we cannot underestimate our own duplicity. The first ears we convince of perceiving a phony, self-serving calling are our own. In our defense is the Bogus Detector we are always ready to activate in someone else's life: If the person I dislike most told me that God was calling her to something, what would I have to say about her motives? What does that suggest about mine?

But the God of heaven and earth is far kinder than we

are. If His word to us is "Let your 'yes' be yes and your 'no' be no" (James 5:12), how much more should we refuse to enhance His own call to us? God's yeses and noes may not align with the ones we want to hear, so this is a risky prospect. Doing something only because we know it's what a Christian would do might turn us into exactly the kind of person we didn't want to be. We might end up seeing those lowlifes in Nineveh repent and be saved, or teaching Sunday School for fourteen years instead of one. We might gain perspective on the distractions and points of pride we thought were our identities, and we might find out that a Christian's real identity is like that of the God who emptied Himself for us (Philippians 2:7). Jesus answered the Father's call to do something utterly undesirable and beneath His dignity, *for the joy set before Him* (Hebrews 12:2). The joy our Father has set before us means that whatever He gives us to do in this life will be more than repaid when we finally hear Him say, "Well done, thou good and faithful servant."

NOT TOO FANCY

Is the Old Testament Misogynist?

Polite Christian company, even the conservative kind, often finds itself a little embarrassed or at least unsure of what to think about what the Bible says about women. Reading the Old Testament can cause as much culture shock as a person's first amble over the glorious California border into Tijuana. It's easy to soothe our disorientation with stereotypes, disgust, and even ridicule. The Old Testament can be explained away by parody (see, for example, *A Year of Biblical Womanhood* by Rachel Held Evans), spin-doctoring (*The Red Tent* by Anita Diamant), or open denunciation (where to begin?). But the difficulty of becoming comfortable in a worldview other than our own is why genuine inquiries should be treated with respect. It is just plain hard to read a book written a long time ago about a culture far, far away. So, did God really think women were icky? Are all the awful things that happened to women in the Old Testament as un-big a deal as the stories can make them sound? Are we just supposed to be okay with King Solomon's one-thousand-member harem? Why don't our beloved Bibles even tell us all those ladies' *names*?

It's important to recognize up front that there isn't anything really unique about the ugly stories of the Bible that feature females. Scripture's accounts of rape, infidelity, injustice, and unfixable situations show how much the times, they aren't a-changing. No sin or human problem is new. There are new ways of judging them and trying to fix them, but the bottom line is that the human experience hasn't changed much in six thousand years, for either women or men.

So let's deal with some real problems. Things seem to start going south for women in Genesis 4:19, where Scripture briefly informs us that a guy named Lamech had two wives, launching what became a pervasive practice. Scripture doesn't bother mentioning that this was contrary to the will of God because that was just covered in the last couple of chapters. We already know that God's intention for marriage is that it be between one husband and one wife, since that's how God created the world He commanded man and woman to populate. In the same way, Scripture offers no moral commentary on Lot's offering of his daughters to a mob of gang rapists. The scenario is so atrociously wrong that we don't need to demand an editorial apology from the Holy Spirit. Lot's reprehensible cowardice speaks for itself. This is how it goes for many scriptural stories of man's inhumanity to man, which often happen to involve women. Objections of the "Why doesn't the Bible say how bad this was?" variety come from reading in the wrong direction. Biblical morality is not absent from these stories. It's our criterion for understanding them.

We also need to put things in cultural perspective and to do so informedly rather than writing off the Old Testament period as one of brutish misogyny. Ceremonial law can be perceived as coming down with particular harshness on women, who spent a lot of their lives unclean. When we read these laws, we should remember that biological realities for women were very different in a time when women spent most of their fertile years pregnant or nursing. In most women, this means extended amenorrhea, which would make all the laws pertaining to menses irrelevant to them. A fair reading would also pay equal attention to more intimate requirements for male cleanliness because the guys had rules too. Finally, we should account for the numerous nonintimate situations that made a person unclean. Sickness caused uncleanness and so did caring for a sick person. Contact with a corpse caused uncleanness in the days before coroners and undertakers. The truth is that most people of both sexes living under ceremonial law spent a lot of time unclean.

We don't like being called unclean, so even if we know it's a little silly to be offended by laws we've never had to keep ourselves, we might still wonder, "What is this woman-shaming doing in our Bible?" The answer is the same. Uncleanness shows the people of God that they are sinners. Sin is unclean, whether or not a ceremonial law is in place to point it out. We should be no more upset by the laws governing cleanness than we are by those horrifying stories we didn't learn in Sunday School, and we should also be no *less* upset. All that bad stuff is in the Bible because the message of forgiveness will never get through to a person who thinks she's pretty good. We need to hear and believe that we are dirty sinners in order to believe that there is forgiveness for us in Christ.

Next problem: why are babies such a big deal? It sounds beyond crazy to us that if a woman's husband dies without a son, his brother is expected to correct the omission. And none of us are going to hand over our housekeeper to have a kid for us, Sarah-style. These fixes aren't peachy, and at least some of them fall under the category of "not endorsed by God Almighty," similar to Lamech and Lot. But a childless woman in the ancient world didn't have any social security. She needed every opportunity to have someone there to care and provide for her, and makeshifting was the way it was done. (There was also an escape clause for those unwilling to participate: Deuteronomy 25:7–10.)

In a certain sense, we can be thankful not to have to live under social mores we now find so distasteful. But we should also look honestly at our own culture's way of doing things. Our time is fine with serial monogamy and some very high-tech forms of parental surrogacy. These approaches to family problems are different from a social perspective, but not an ethical one. We are not the sinless generation licensed for stone-casting when it comes to marriage and baby trouble. Our spouse-swapping and surrogacies may appear cleaner, but the intimate integrity of both men and women is still violated, both in our attempts to keep marriage interesting and in many contemporary processes of finagling a baby out of God. The Old Testament didn't have a good solution, and neither do we.

Finally, there is the problem of recognition. All those lists of names, and nary a female in sight! Let's assume that we're reading lists of names for some reason other than counting up the women, and get on to the explanation. Nearly all human genealogies are traced through the male line, including our own, just because a birth announcement for little Johnny Schmidt-Schultz-Schwarzkopf-Schroedinger isn't practical. Tracing through the female line is also a dubious honor. That way of doing things operates under the principle of *mama's baby, papa's maybe*, which isn't the nicest way to remember a family's ladies. Counting by dads gives the dads an incentive to keep their names clean, which is good news for the whole family. It's always in women's best interests to keep men on their best behavior, and on balance, patrilinear family histories have advantages for everyone.

So the Old Testament is a place where bad things happen to bad and good people, lots of them women. Ancient Near East ladies find themselves in bad situations: they are taken advantage of, they have their honor stolen and their futures ruined, they deal with the physical and social taxes on their complicated biology, nobody remembers their names, and they still have to pick up after everybody. Sounds pretty familiar, except that the families of rape victims aren't allowed to kill rapists anymore. As the Old Testament might say, "There is nothing new under the sun" (Ecclesiastes 1:9).

We could leave it at that, but let's be a little more fair. The Old Testament also speaks of women with a tenderness and sensitivity we might not expect from a supposedly dark age. Job's daughters are so beautiful that, unconstrained by the demands of history, we are told their names—Jemimah, Keziah, and Keren-happuch—while we never get to meet his seven boys. The treasured lamb of the poor man in Nathan's parable was "like a daughter to him." A daughter! Not the prized son we might expect, and then again, anyone who has ever held the surpassingly precious gift of a baby girl knows why Nathan puts it this way.

God Almighty, famously known as "our Father in heaven," repeatedly describes Himself in the Psalms and the prophetic books with images that could not be more exclusively female: a woman in labor and a nursing mother. Do men find these descriptions offensive or discriminatory? If they do, they complain about it a lot less than some women do. But they would also be just as wrong in their complaints as those women are. With metaphors like these, God shows that the female experience is thoroughly human. A person doesn't need to be a mother to understand why God would describe His surpassing pain and superlative love for us as being like a mother's for her child. And yet the pinnacle of all love is the Son of Man pouring out His own life for the life of the world. How impoverished we would be to seek only ourselves in Scripture when what God would have us find there is Himself. When God talks about His Old Testament people, He says, "My Delight Is in Her" (Isaiah 62:4). If we can understand and believe that, our ears are in the right place to hear the rest of what a God who loves and delights in us has to say.

What Would Lydia Do?

There is nothing a ladies' Bible study loves talking about like "Women of the Bible." Lydia is a favorite: a professional in a respected and profitable trade who came to faith, was baptized with her household, and opened her home to Paul and Silas.

From this briefest of biographies—Lydia receives only three verses in Scripture—our day has extrapolated divine endorsement for two of its most treasured beliefs: God wants women to have lucrative, high-profile professions, and God wants women to be leaders in the Church!

If the point of Lydia's appearance in Scripture is to teach women how to live, an earlier day may well have extrapolated something different. Another time might have learned from Lydia that even a woman driven by a desire for wealth, a consuming sense of mannish ambition, and an inappropriate intrusion into public life to the unavoidable neglect of her home and family may be won to faith by the transforming Word of God.

Which set of extrapolators is correct? Neither. God does not have Lydia moonlight in Scripture to give us an important lesson in sex roles. He tells us about Lydia to show how His Holy Church grows through the preaching of the Gospel of Christ. Scripture offers no judgment on the personal life of either Lydia or the jailer who appears later in Acts 16. Not every person in Scripture is there to teach us how to live, except in one regard: each of them demonstrates that the only way to life eternal is forgiveness in Christ, and the only way to forgiveness is repentance, and the only way to repent is to begin by admitting that we are sinners.

So, Lydia repented of her sins, whatever those sins were, and she and her household were baptized into the saving death of Christ. That is why the Holy Spirit wants the Church to know her. She is surely an example of repentance. But we can't be sure about any examples the rest of her life may offer. We simply don't have that information. To pretend that we do is disingenuous and arrogant.

The same may be said of Phoebe (two verses), Priscilla (seven verses, always with her husband, Aquila), Junia (one verse), Chloe (one verse), or any of the other drive-by female personalities of the Early Church. Each of these women have become victims of wild contemporary deductions for the justification of every cause of female interest. We might as well devise an elaborate ethos based on the female names mentioned in one random parish's Sunday bulletin. Laboring for the Church is a blessed practice and a natural manifestation of Christian belief.

But it is precisely because that manifestation of belief is natural that we should not find it surprising. What *would* be surprising is a New Testament in which no ladies' names happened to pop up, even as a church bulletin that didn't name Bernice as this month's cleaner and thank Debbie for the VBS snacks and remind everyone to call Diana with newsletter updates would strike us as very odd. What kind of church isn't kept afloat by the tireless efforts of its ladies?

Of course, there are women in the New Testament: they are half of the race for whom Christ died. They can't be avoided, as many a cookie-sneaking boy can testify.

The history of the Early Church as we receive it in Scripture is both authoritative and personal because the Church is both our authority and our corporate person. As persons, we always remember those who are dear to us, and into every life a dear female almost certainly falls. The life of the Church is no exception. We remember our foremothers in the faith not to make a sociopolitical point, but simply because they are our mothers and our lives would not be the same without them. It does both them and us a disservice to disregard their highest commendation for the purpose of making virtues out of our own necessities or desires. God honors Lydia, Phoebe, Priscilla, and all the rest by upholding them as models of repentance, faith, and Christian duty. We would turn them into mascots for irrelevant, transient, and self-serving causes.

There is one other problem with extrapolation—its necessity for making the points pride wishes to make. Only the sturdiest of imaginations could hold that a St. Junia sits among the holy apostolic band, which Scripture defines clearly to the exclusion of such a person, or that the prophesying daughters of Philip make the case for women's ordination two thousand years later. These contentions come at the price of extravagant speculation as to what really happened. They also slander those who must have maliciously suppressed the truth in the lengthy interval. They put no confidence in the Holy Spirit to communicate through His inspired Word. Finally, they deny the integrity of the Church, her love for her children, and her desire for what is best for them.

Christians count all but loss so that we may obtain Christ[21]—including, if need be, our pet causes, our worldly "opportunities," our personal interests, and our comforts. We would like to overlook the difficulty of daily repentance and death to our sins in the interest of progressing to a more advanced spirituality. Somehow spiritual advancement always amounts to our getting to spend more time on the things we like, and calling it "stewardship" or "service." This shows how seriously we underestimate the power of sin. Our flesh believes that we'll be really serving God when we're finally getting to do exactly what we want.

But the economy demands something other than all of us working in quality control at a chocolate factory. Therefore, it stands to reason that our deepest desires are not always equivalent to our greatest possible acts of Christian service. What Jesus wants from us is repentance, every day of our lives. He would rather have us be holy than self-actualized. It is better for us to die daily to sin than to open that cookie shop or write that novel or finish that degree. Seeing Lydia mainly as a model of female mercantilism (plus Jesus!) reduces her to a token and disregards the most important thing about her and the reason God wants us to make her acquaintance: she was a sinner who responded to apostolic preaching with humility, repented of her sins, and clung to the promises of Christ. Blessed are we if we follow that example.

---

[21] "One Thing's Needful" (LSB 536).

Jesus the Feminist?

Was Jesus a feminist? No. Feminism is a social movement conceived in the early twentieth century. Jesus lived in the first century.

Okay, that's not what you meant. Did Jesus treat women fairly and with respect? Did He end discrimination?

Well, those are two different questions. Let's start with the second. Jesus did not end discrimination between men and women. He discriminated between them Himself. He did not choose a single woman as one of the Twelve, which can hardly have been an accident. If His mission had included proactively ending differentiation between the sexes, He would have needed a number of women to equal the men in His inner circle, as our own antidiscrimination laws demand. There were no women present at His transfiguration. He was not baptized by a woman. In His public ministry, the colleagues and deployed staff He chose were male.

Was Jesus accommodating the norms of His time? This kind of compliance would have been totally out of His character. Jesus violated cultural norms constantly. He spoke against the traditions of the rabbis and repeatedly broke them personally. He touched the unclean, He hung around with sinners, and He deliberately offended the authorities of His cultural community. He gave the gifts of God's kingdom to Gentiles and healed the son of a Roman overlord. He spoke civilly to a Samaritan (who happened to be a woman) and defended a person caught in the very act of adultery (who also happened to be a woman). But He never appointed a woman to a position of authority or a public office. Jesus had many agenda items that were unthinkable to the people to whom He was sent, but obliterating the social differences between men and women was not one of them.

Does this make Him a misogynist? The women of His day were in a better position to judge that than we are, and they didn't seem to think so. Mary and Martha of Bethany welcomed Him to their home and cherished His friendship. Mary Magdalene, Susanna, Joanna the wife of Chuza, and many other women followed Him and supported Him with their own money. Salome, Joanna, and a variety of Marys are named as having come to His tomb to care for His body after His death. Women aren't really in the habit of voluntarily doing nice things for misogynists. It's hard to imagine them offering all these services, unasked, to a guy who treated them like donkeys. These women had no personal obligation to Jesus. Mary and Martha were close to Him before He healed their brother. Although Mary Magdalene's devotion to Him may have originated in His freeing her from demonic possession, her response of love far exceeds that of most people Jesus healed, who disappear from the narrative after receiving the favor.

In fact, what we see in the Gospels is Jesus extending kindness, grace, and basic human respect to every woman who crosses His path. When a woman with a hemorrhage touches His robe in trust, He does not lash out at her for transferring her uncleanness to Him, but He heals her and commends her faith. When women with deservedly horrible reputations come to Him in ashamed repentance, He holds them up as examples of faithfulness. When a Gentile woman begs Him to heal her demon-possessed daughter, He banters with her as a person of intellectual parity and listens to her cogent argument for her belief that He will heal someone outside the Abrahamic promise. And yet, for the high praise He affords these people, He does not even see to it that history knows their names. Their value is their faith, not their "personal identities." This, again, is no accident. God knows that the heart of man, and also woman, always seeks earthly fame. But it is more important for our names to be in the Lamb's Book of Life than known to the world.

Furthermore, we do not see women vilified in the life of Jesus. He does not grant them public offices; neither are they responsible for His public execution. He is not betrayed by a woman, tried by women, sentenced by a woman, tortured by women, or crucified by women. In the Gospels, we see women forgiven, healed, fed, taught, and personally spoken to by Jesus, but never belittled, scorned, or reviled.

But isn't it belittling, scorning, and reviling to have excluded them from His public ministry? Anyone who would answer yes to this question is looking for the wrong thing from Jesus. Jesus came to serve and to give His life as a ransom for many, not to create job opportunities and even things out and give women the recognition of which they've supposedly been robbed for all these centuries. He came to forgive sinners, a category of people that includes women (along with Gentiles and overlords and everybody else). If the forgiveness of sins, appeasement of God's holy wrath, salvation from death, and rescue from everlasting condemnation are not enough from Jesus, nothing will be.

If the Jesus in Scripture is not the Jesus we want, we are no different from the Jews waiting for an earthly messiah to overthrow the Romans. We are the crowd shouting "Crucify Him!" because He failed to save us from what we imagined we wanted ourselves saved—our annoyances rather than our sins. We see ourselves as victims and not as perpetrators. We're not as concerned about our own damning sin as we are about the people we don't like and our pet causes. There cannot be a more destructive approach to life and faith. It is the failure to fear God. It is the belief that we know better. Thinking this way will kill us. Our real problem is never oppression, deprivation, or injustice but the *cause* of all those things. That cause is sin, and nobody's sin is more dangerous to us than our own.

When mothers bring their children to Jesus for a blessing, He doesn't tell the disciples to take the kids for the afternoon so the poor moms can have a break for once. When Peter's mother-in-law begins to wait on the people present after she is raised from her sickbed, Jesus doesn't tell her to take it easy and that they'll find their own cheese and crackers. He doesn't offer that sharp Syro-Phoenician lady a professorship. When the myrrh-bearers report the resurrection to the cowardly disciples, Jesus doesn't show up, depose the guys, and promote the deserving ladies to the apostolic positions instead. For some reason, the women who knew Him loved Him and freely chose to serve Him anyway. Maybe they could see things two thousand years of growing human ingratitude have blurred.

FIAT MIHI, FIAT LUX[22]

When the heirs of the Reformation look through our Bibles for our own highly favored lady, Mary is our last resort. There is something about her that doesn't count. She is too high and holy to be a handmaiden, too maidenly to be pregnant, and too pregnant to be high and holy. A lady so great with child doesn't do much for those of us who aren't great with children, and if your child was perfect baby Jesus, who *wouldn't* be a great mother? She is too worshiped by our Roman Catholic cousins and too girl-next-door to be worth fighting about. It would be a lot easier to get back to Miriam and Priscilla.

Hard things have big payoffs, though. Clicking "Ignore" on Mary's friendship request is cutting off our nose to spite our faith. She is not, as the Roman Church teaches, the co-redemptrix of humanity. Christ alone is the world's Redeemer from sin. But Mary is the "small *r*" redemption of every earthly thing that went wrong for women when the first woman went wrong.

The Eve/Adam situation is a bit jumbly. Eve started the eating but Adam gets the blame. "Sin came into the world through one man" (Romans 5:12). "As in Adam all die, so also in Christ shall all be made alive" (1 Corinthians 15:22). But

---

[22] Let it be to me; Let there be light.

Eve was deceived, not Adam (1 Timothy 2:14), so where does she end up in all this?

God is not one to leave equations crooked. The wages of Adam's sin are paid by Christ on the cross, but the complication of Eve's involvement is also accounted for. One woman's unbelief is counterbalanced by one woman's belief. One woman doubts what God said, and one woman trusts. One woman submits to the message of the fallen angel, and one submits to the message of the holy angel. Eve apostatizes with silence and active disobedience, and the door to humanity's condemnation swings open. Mary assents with her confession: "Let it be to me according to your word" (Luke 1:38). She receives the ultimate gift of God, and light blazes through a doorway open to humanity's salvation. It is God's Son who saves, and Eve's daughter who is that Son's mother.

We should not be surprised that the fallen angel works so hard for his revenge against this new Eve. He has attacked her from every angle. In her own life, it was easy enough: nobody's nice to a knocked-up teenager, and nobody forgets. When the cruelty of living memory ran out, the deceiver made the humble handmaiden into the glorious goddess she never sought to be. He strains the faith of the faithful by adding to what has been divinely revealed about Mary. He drains the faith of others, diverting them from trust in an awe-full God to His more approachable mother. Satan has done his damnedest to make Mary a caricature, a scandal, a lie, and a joke.

He does this because he is scared. The Seed of the woman is his undoing, so he must undo her. If he cannot make her our idol, the devil would have us believe that Mary is worth nothing to anyone because no other woman on earth can be the Virgin Mother. But the truth is that Mary is all things to all women. She is the virgin of virgins and the mother of mothers, and still more than that. She is the girl with the ruined reputation who's got to get through life anyway. She is the widow, crumpled bereft at the cross. She is the wife who needs protection, the mother with a child she can't understand, and the woman at the mercy of the men around her. She is the lady who didn't get the life she'd imagined. She is the ever-flummoxed female. She is the believer.

She is also the mother of God. No amount of caution against human susceptibility to satanic lies makes it wise or faithful to downplay the whole truth about Mary. She is not the consort of God; neither is she just another miserable biped. The union of God and man begins literally with her, in her physical body, as a fact of history and biology, and that fact has consequences. Jesus Christ, true God, begotten of the Father from eternity, is also true man, born of the Virgin Mary. The mystery of the incarnation is that *God has a mom*. That His relationship with her would be different from the one He has with the rest of us is only human. Clothed with the sun and crowned with stars, a woman roars in the humiliating agony of childbirth (Revelation 12:1–2). The only thing that could make less sense would be God dying in naked anguish on a government cross. Like children and parents everywhere, Jesus and His mother have more than a little in common.

Mary's entire person comes down to one thing: *Let it*

be to me according to Your word. This little sentence is the essence of Christian faith. *Let it be to me according to Your word,* and the Word became flesh and dwelt within her. The serpent asks, "Did God actually say . . . ?" and Eve falls silent. The angel says, "You will conceive in your womb and bear a son, and you shall call His name Jesus." Mary answers, "Let it be to me according to Your word." And God said, "Let there be light," and the true light, which gives light to everyone, came into the world.

If the answer to Adam's ultimate, cosmic culpability is Christ, the answer to Eve's secondary, human culpability is Mary. This is what Paul means when he says, "There is no male and female, for you are all one in Christ Jesus" (Galatians 3:28). Scripture is not saying that there are no longer two classifications of people; but that in Christ, there are no second-class people, regardless of what happened in the beginning.

The wreck at the beginning has been undone. Every disastrous second has been replayed and unmade. We are one with Christ because He was one with one of us. Eve's pride is countered in Mary's humility. Eve's disobedience is countered in Mary's submission. Eve's doubt is countered in Mary's belief. Eve's sin is canceled in Mary's Son. She has gotten a Man, the Lord. Let it be to us according to His Word.

SINS OF THE FATHERS

Misogyny is one of the world's favorite grenades to launch at Christianity, and the great men of the Early Church are an especially cherished target. But even the world knows better than to negotiate with terrorists, so we might question the propriety of addressing this allegation at all. If the Fathers of the Early Church made statements that were truly misogynistic, doesn't airing their sin fall squarely into the category of uncharity? Love keeps no record of wrong. This should incline us to caution, for the Commandments permit neither dishonoring fathers nor damaging reputations.

History, however, records right and wrong alike, and there are those in the world who do not claim the same Fathers we do. Rather than loving these men, the world hates them and wants nothing more than to destroy their reputations. In quoting the Fathers' purported misogyny, the world wishes to slander them and discredit their work. This again steers us to caution, since the words selected by those outside the faith will surely be the most unflattering available, not only taken out of immediate context but also torn from the greater language of the Church.

But swaying our uneasy question is the critical truth that what sounds one way to the sinner falls differently on the ear of the saint. What would we say to those who slander our Fathers and urge us to join in? We would say, perhaps, "Make your case, for we love our Fathers and see only good in them, even as only good is spoken of us to our Father by Him whose name we have been given. Let us see whether you have judged rightly."

"Misogynistic" statements of the Fathers are so familiar as to render quotation dull. Who can come out of a Christian liberal arts institution without having heard Tertullian and Chrysostom on Eve's sin, Augustine on woman as temptress, Jerome on woman as just plain icky, Aquinas on feminine inferiority, Luther on a woman's broad fundament, and Knox on her monstrous regiment? Rather than giving more airtime to this tired loop of sound bites, we will deal with broader objections. The offensive sentiments can be grouped into a few categories:

> Eve caused the fall into sin.
>
> Women cause men to sin sexually.
>
> Women are unclean, naturally inferior to men, and unfit for the tasks of men.

The first statement, that Eve caused the fall into sin, is entirely true. A Christian woman who hears the horrific story of our great mother's temptation would be a fool if her heart were not given over to sadness, shame, and holy fear upon hearing it. It is little wonder that women find it offensive, for it always offends us to hear that we are sinners. Eve's fall is a warning to every woman to repent and cast her hope (as Eve did) on the Seed of the woman, who would redeem her. Furthermore, Scripture devotes considerable time to the guilt of Adam as well as the guilt of Eve. Whatever might be said of Eve's guilt neither denies nor mitigates the culpability of Adam. It does us good to be reminded that woman stands at the singularity of sin's black hole. There is a sense in which Eve, the bearer of the Bearer of God who perhaps shouldn't have been involved in the first place, can come out of the story looking rather better. The Christian response to sin is humility and contrition, never lashing out in self-defense. To hear of Eve is to hear of each of us.

The second statement, that women are a factor in men's sexual sins, is generally true, since men are generally subject to sexual temptation and always sinful. What may a Christian woman take away from such statements? That she should be scrupulous in her own charity toward her brother's fight with sin. Her dress and demeanor should be humble; her beauty should proceed from her character (1 Peter 3). This calls for wisdom since a myriad of questions of culture and etiquette menace the matter with their unquantifiable demands. There can be no answer to them all, except that the Christian woman should be willing to bow as low as she would to our Lord to receive the mantle of modesty.

Replying to questions of sexual temptation with accusations of male perversion and irresponsibility is unbecoming of a Christian lady, for the Christian position (particularly that of the woman) is always one of humility and charity. Responding with meekness and renewed attention to one's personal behavior does not exonerate anyone who may be guilty of a sinful response to female beauty. That is his problem. It does a lady no harm to wear a longer skirt or give him a wider berth. We are all lowered by meretricious dress and behavior. The pious requests of Christian men for modesty among Christian women are far from oppressive.

The third statement, regarding the inferiority, unfitness, and uncleanness of women, begins in an area which has ever been difficult ground for people of faith: scientific knowledge. If there is one advantage the children of this age have over the Church Fathers, it is science (a dangerous advantage to have, as we have also learned). For all their wisdom, the ancients and most of their spiritual heirs did not have access to some simple biological facts. Such misunderstandings may account for certain characterizations of man, woman, and even the unborn. Here we are also carried toward secular philosophy (rooted as it is in scientific knowledge), a world more fraught, if possible, than Christian ethics. Some Fathers were particularly influenced by Plato, Aristotle, or others of the Greek pantheon of thinkers, all of whom, like so many pagans and other followers of the devil, held a rather low opinion of women.

In lieu of tumbling down this troublesome rabbit hole, however, we may turn to a father less ancient but at least as vulnerable to the recent feminist charge of misogyny. In 1901, G. K. Chesterton wrote in the journal *The Speaker*, "Whether woman is structurally different to man is a matter of physical science, whether she is superior or inferior or equal is not a matter of physical science; it is a question of what you happen to want." If what one wants is a man, one will always be disappointed and disgusted when considering a woman. She is by definition unmanly and lacking in *vir*tue (Latin for *man*). Compared to a man, a woman will and must always fall short.

It is to the advantage of man and woman alike to know this. Refusing to face facts about sex differences in terms of physical strength, emotional proclivity, and intellectual inclination ends, for example, with women fighting wars while a host of men who have never considered cultivating in themselves courage or chivalry watch basketball from the couch. Men have had their birthright swiped for a bowl of feminist pottage (*You know where the kitchen is! Make it yourself, pig!*), while women are blessed to have their most peculiar and therefore precious gifts protected by inexorable facts of biology, which callously exclude men from pregnancy and lactation.

Speaking of pregnancy and lactation, what is to be made of uncleanness? The same that is to be made of Eve's sin and woman's sex appeal, which is to say, it is a fact. Humans are an unclean race, as anyone who has ever provided physical care for a human knows. Women, who have the particular joy of manufacturing other unclean humans, can hardly expect the process to go off without any spills. We can take some consolation in the fact that it is also usually women who clean them up.

The foregoing effort grants our opponents the courtesy of treating their objections as worthy. Anyone who judges the Church Fathers by a handful of amputated statements and purely personal criteria is unqualified to speak to patristic credibility or integrity. True misogyny would explicitly or effectively exclude women from salvation in Christ. There is not one Church Father of whom this can be said, regardless of whether his opinions on women would be welcome at a contemporary barbecue.

This ultimately is the measure of the world's perception of not only the Fathers but the Christian faith as a whole. Those who reject Christ find every part of Him reprehensible, including His spokesmen. Misogyny is a fashionable villain of our time and the only reason statements that attracted no special attention for centuries have suddenly become widely known. If none of the famous patristic sound bites about women existed, the world would still malign the Church as misogynistic for her confession that virginity or marriage (and, where God grants it, motherhood) are the proper and honorable callings of women.

One of feminism's first orders of business is to nurture in its disciples an unflattering fault of femininity: the reflexive taking of exaggerated offense. To ears so trained, every statement negates its converse, denies its omissions, and implies insult. This reaction is neither rational nor Christian. Christians must be willing to hear of their sins, since anyone who cannot hear of her own sin cannot repent of it. Our increasingly facile and recalcitrant society would rather have its feelings hurt than hear an honest criticism or a good argument. Such pseudo-reasoning requires exposure and little else. Lessons like this are the debt we owe our Fathers.

Hey Mister Pastor Man

The ordination of men has, until very recently, been a straightforward practice, because Scripture is clear on the point:

> I do not permit a woman to teach or to exercise authority over a man; rather, she is to remain quiet. (1 Timothy 2:12)

> As in all the churches of the saints, the women should keep silent in the churches. For they are not permitted to speak, but should be in submission, as the Law also says. (1 Corinthians 14:33b–34)

> Therefore an overseer must be above reproach, *the husband of one wife*, sober-minded, self-controlled, respectable, hospitable, able to teach. (1 Timothy 3:2; emphasis added)

It's hard to argue with such plain statements; so hard, in fact, that the only way to get around them is to reject the authority of their source. Churches that ordain women as pastors deny that God really meant those old, cold, moldy words of Scripture.

This may seem harmless. The whole business sounds suspiciously like mean old-timey people's bad ideas about life in general. But that isn't what history shows. From ancient times, most religions have had girl priests and girl gods. The Old Testament people of God were surrounded by people who worshiped the Mesopotamian goddesses Anat, Innana, and/or Asherah (they overlap quite a bit). The New Testament Church grew up in the lands of Artemis (Ephesus), Aphrodite (Corinth), and Cybele (Galatia).

Priestesses and distinctly female religious observances were so common in the ancient world as to be unremarkable. Jeremiah 44 talks specifically about the women of Israel worshiping a regional goddess (their husbands knew but didn't care). Self-preference is nothing new, and false religion back in the day was as shrewd as it has ever been. A temple with lady gods and staff will always bring in the ladies. People of our time have become more honest about their false god of choice, cutting out the middlemen in favor of the efficient practice of self-worship. In the case of half the human race, this amounts again to goddess worship, as our own disposable razors testify. The exclusively masculine holy office is not a holdover from a less inclusive time. It actually distinguishes the religion of God from the religions of the gods, made male and female in the image of the humans who dreamed them up.

The question of who talks in church also seems pretty far removed from the forgiveness of sins by Jesus' death on the cross, so why make a big deal of it? Just ordain the ladies. The trouble is that once we start excising things from Scripture, it's hard to tell where to stop. This is why ecclesiastical outfits that ordain women end up with Bibles that look like snowflakes cut by preschoolers. Once you take out all the ridiculous stuff—talking donkeys and guys inside whales, all the rules about sex, the dead getting raised and the certainty of things unseen—there's no point in keeping what's left on your nightstand. Somehow there are still people drawing paychecks for their expertise in Bible-shredding,[23] but the Promised Land, like any personal possession, can only be sold once. The churches that have cashed out their share of the family farm scramble to make something of the diminishing returns, while the rest of us deal with the damage done by the sale.

The world says, "What do you mean, women *can't* be pastors?" The child of God answers, "Why would they want to be?" There may be some arguing about respect or status or opportunity, but this can all be exposed as artificial. The pastor is not a person or Christian of better quality. If he were truly respected, he'd be better paid, and outside the Church, he is not respected at all. Attainment of the office itself is no considerable proof of intellect or talent, as the existence of both mediocre pastors and more-demanding fields of expertise demonstrates. Martin Luther argued in one of his most ecumenically beloved quotations that a milkmaid at her work is as pleasing to God as a priest or monk. The reason some women get upset over women's ordination is simple coveting. They want what has been given to someone else, and they don't want someone else to have something they are unable to have. The complaint is borne of a phony injury to pride, the part of us that most needs to be injured.

In the Old Testament, only the descendants of Aaron were priests, and only the tribe of Levi served in the temple.

---

23 It is worthy of notice that at least a plurality of the Bible-shredders are men. A bottle of Glenmorangie in a womanless room would probably evince an honest statement from most men on the topic of ladies in pastor suits. Women's ordination is and always has been the doing of women, fueled where necessary by the desire of men to have some quiet, and we will address it as such.

Somehow, Naphtali and Gad never felt a need to prove their worth by demanding ecclesiastical jobs for themselves. The Church has always been full of men who are not pastors and are totally fine with not having been given that calling. The way for each of us to please God and serve our neighbor is to faithfully perform the work He has given us, and pastoral ministry is simply not work He has given women to do. That so many women refuse to gracefully accept the order God has made for His people is far greater evidence of female small-mindedness than willing submission to His Word would be. It's like being mad that today is someone else's birthday or hating a pretty girl for her thin ankles. Were the case taken before Solomon, advocates of women's ordination would have him abolish the pastoral office altogether rather than give it over to its true mother, the Church.

The Law of God is His revealed will, and it is holy, good, and wise. If God loved us enough to die for our sins, surely we can also trust Him not to be wasting women's talents, squashing our identities, or hiding from us behind intolerably male pastors. The world would force an appetite for prestige, promiscuity, and violence into women under the guise of equality, but the Church is where women are praised precisely for their resistance to these indecent things. In exhorting women to quietness and chastity (1 Peter 3:1–6), Scripture reminds us that women often do a particularly good job of living out these virtues, and that the whole Church benefits from their examples of faithfulness. In the same way that women are honored to take up this charge in God's service, it is their honor to say, "We'd rather have things the way God set them up, so if you men will kindly keep this place in order, we'll know we're in our Father's house, and we'll be glad to help out wherever we're needed." The true Church does not ordain women; neither will women of the true Church permit themselves to be ordained, or submit to anyone who teaches contrary to Scripture.

Every woman who refuses to recognize any authority in the Church except that which God has set in place stands against the world, the flesh, and the devil. She is the first line of defense against the world's intended takeover of the Church because she will not allow the world's ways into the Church. If the people of God will not be subject to the world's philosophical fads and social dogmas, they are also primed to resist other intrusions. They will reject a life driven by the pursuit of pleasure. They will reject the imperialistic claim of science to be our new god. They will reject cruelty, violence, deprivation, and every act of human evil, as human history shows.

The allocation of women to men by means of hut-raiding and hair-dragging was the social circumstance under which Christianity found more than one enclave of our fallen race. It was the Church that drove savagery out of human society and replaced it with the values that protect women best: chaste monogamy, charitable provision for the needy, and a preference for peaceable resolution of conflicts. *These things are the will of God, revealed in His good, wise, and holy Law.* All of this was accomplished under the leadership of men who trusted God too much to follow their own appetites and loved people too much to give them over to their own sin. These men submitted to the Law of God even though it often meant giving up what they personally wanted. Women do the same when they submit to God's ordering of His Church. Sometimes it means mortifying our own flesh, and sometimes it means refusing to be complicit in the sin of others. But it is always an act of faith and faithfulness to believe what God says and to insist upon it.

God has spoken by His prophets. John the Baptist, the greatest among those born of women, testified, "[Christ] must increase, but I must decrease" (John 3:30). It is the opposite testimony of those who, brazenly claiming prophetic authority, would devour those in the way of the place they want. Considering how often Scripture warns us about false prophets, the regularity with which claims are made on the prophetic office is astonishing. The Old Testament Church had a test and a punishment for a false prophet:

> "But the prophet who presumes to speak a word in My name that I have not commanded him to speak, or who speaks in the name of other gods, that same prophet shall die." And if you say in your heart, "How may we know the word that the LORD has not spoken?"—when a prophet speaks in the name of the LORD, if the word does not come to pass or come true, that is a word that the LORD has not spoken; the prophet has spoken it presumptuously. (Deuteronomy 18:20–22; emphasis added)

On the other side of the New Testament, the Early Church also had a test for prophets:

> Whosoever, therefore, comes and teaches you all these things that have been said before, receive him. But if the teacher himself turns and teaches

> *another doctrine to the destruction of this, hear*
> *him not. . . .* But not every one who speaks in
> the Spirit is a prophet; but only if he holds the
> ways of the Lord. Therefore from their ways
> shall the false prophet and the prophet be
> known. (Didache 11:1, 8; emphasis added)

Many self-identified prophets add to or subtract from what Scripture teaches about the role of women in the Church, but everyone who speaks as a prophet is subject to judgment. It has always been the Church's job to discern true prophets from false ones, and the test is the prophecy itself. The ordination of women is in direct opposition to the revealed Word of God. It is *speaking in the name of other gods*, the ancient ones against whom God warned His people and the iGod of the present. It is teaching something *other than* and *destructive to* what has been said before. It causes division in the Church and leads people astray. It is the perfect example of a false prophecy.

But if heresy is an insufficient disincentive, there is still the problem of tackiness. The only thing more embarrassing than being told to move down lower is to be informed that one is at a table to which she was never invited at all. The marriage feast of the Lamb is coming, and we will all be expected to dress appropriately (Matthew 22:11–13). Those of us to whom the preaching office has not been given are still entrusted with the eternal and everyday truth of Scripture. Never has there been a time when it was more important for a woman of God to tell her sister, "Girlfriend, that stole is just not *you*."

IT'S VERY PERSONAL

What Is God Trying to Tell You?

Two things: You are a sinner. You are forgiven in Christ. That's it.

That's the simple version, but 'tis a gift to be simple, and here's what we can learn from it: God is not a cosmic micromanager of human life. He made each of us a free agent with regard to our earthly decisions, and that is a generous gift. It means that any question lacking a moral dimension does not have a right or wrong answer. Within the Law of God and the law of the authorities that God has set in place, the people of God may live how they want to live.

Sounds good, right? But there's a backward part of us that doesn't want that. There's a part that wants to be able to say,

"The pay raise was God's way of telling me that I should stay at this job."

"That thing he said about kimchi was how I knew God wanted me to break up with him."

"After we met with the realtor, it was so clear that this was the home God had chosen for us."

"Finding those Danskos on eBay was such a God thing."

"If God didn't want us to eat animals, he wouldn't have made them out of meat."

Okay, that last one was Homer Simpson. Maybe that's a clue that attaching a divine sanction to decisions about our personal lives isn't divinely sanctioned. Christian freedom allows us to make decisions, but it also means that the credit for them is ours. God loves us, but that does not mean that He sits in judgment over what we have for breakfast. We are free to eat cream cheese on a whole-wheat bagel (even GMO wheat!), or scrambled eggs (they don't have to be free range!), or a doughnut (YES!).

We should thank God for His provision for us, and thank Him even more for when He generously allows us to choose among differing provisions. But we don't get to pump up our own confidence in the decisions we make by putting His name on them. God showed His love for us in this, that while we were yet sinners, Christ died for us (Romans 5:8). He does not show His love for us by anxiously wringing His all-creating hands while we deliberate the merits of the black dress vis-à-vis the hibiscus print. For this we should also thank Him because there is no way of knowing "what God wants" when it comes to any question outside of Christian morality as we have learned it from Scripture.

Christian freedom means that our *no wrong answer* decisions truly have no wrong answer. God is not dropping sneaky clues that we'd better pick up on if we want to avoid lifelong disaster. Which line of work to pursue, whether to sell one car, which set of grandkids to relocate near, whether to try to adopt right now—these are all questions to be approached with thought and prayer, but not with the expectation that there's a lightning bolt with our name on it if we choose the six instead of the half dozen (or, for that matter, the rock rather than the hard place).

Taking ownership of our decisions also protects us

against putting our human shortsightedness on God's account. Did God really want me to enroll in the graduate program I had to quit three months later when Grammie got sick? What was going on when the convertible the Almighty intended for me got T-boned? And how do I turn down a meet-up request from a guy who is convinced that God led him to my eHarmony profile? When we make decisions, it's too easy to spin *what I want* or *what feels right to me* or even *what I feel like I have to do* into *God's will for my life*. Humanity has an ugly track record of atrocities ostensibly committed in the holy name of God. Our fallen race on both sides of the Thirty Years' War imagined it to have been a God-pleasing effort. Are we so much wiser than our forerunners in the faith that we can trust our own readings of God's mind?

God *does* love us and He has a wonderful plan for our lives. He is *not* a sadistic enigmatologist looking down on us like we're rats in a laboratory maze blundering into cheeseless cul-de-sacs. Everybody benefits when credit goes where it is due. God gives us the ability to reason and the freedom to make choices in this life. Good, bad, or inconsequential, those choices are ours, and we don't have a right to legitimize them with a retroactive divine imprimatur. A hymn puts it another way: "What more can He say than to you He has said / Who unto the Savior for refuge have fled?"[24] God has already told us everything we need to know to live a life pleasing to Him. It is "laid for your faith in His excellent Word!"[25] Or as a T-shirt from the nineties might counsel us,

---

24, 25   "How Firm A Foundation" (LSB 728:1).

Life is salvation by grace through faith for Christ's sake. The rest is just Christian freedom.

So which of those two houses, cars, schools, jobs, princes, or doughnuts is the right one? Either (as long as one of the jobs isn't "assassin"). The real message there is that anyone who gets to choose between two of anything is blessed. What is God trying to tell you today? That you are a sinner, and that you are forgiven in Christ. In fact, that's what He's trying to tell you every day of your life. What you do with the rest of it on that basis is totally—*totally*—up to you.

Marthas, Marthas

Once there was a church kitchen where the food was good, the work was hard, and the lights never went out on an unwiped surface. The ladies of that kitchen tended it ferociously. They covered acres of counter with dough from scratch and burned their arms on the stove hood and just plain showed up for stuff. They ate last and fast and reported right back to start the cleanup. They didn't notice when diners started heading out toward the lighted stained glass windows because it was their job to make sure the kitchen would be ready for its next big performance.

There was another church kitchen where the food was good and the work was hard, and the love went even deeper than that of a lady for her kitchen. It was for what had brought them there to begin with—not that the people of God needed food or service or good times together, but that they needed GOD. They had come to hear Him, and weren't the ladies people of God? They strained their ears for a minute or two, then looked at one another, and one of them said, "We'll clean it up before we leave." They turned off the lights on a dirty kitchen because God Himself was present in His proclaimed Word, where He had promised to be, which happened at that moment not to be in the kitchen.

This isn't to say that the ladies of the first kitchen didn't love God. They loved Him so much that the church kitchen was a place where they didn't growl or resent or keep record of who didn't show up for stuff, which is to say, they resisted one of womanity's greatest temptations. They loved God so deeply that they cooked for His people and washed the gummy forks and sent the leftovers home with the pastor as a matter of course. Like so many good Christian ladies, they probably didn't know what to make of Luke 10.

It's hard for a woman who has ever had full responsibility for hosting or serving to understand the sisters of Bethany. Jesus commends Mary and reprimands Martha, so we know what the right answer is, but it can still be hard to see how the numbers add up. The kitchen ladies are secretly wondering, "But how was everybody going to eat? What did the disciples think of Martha? What were they thinking of Mary, the one woman crashing and thereby ruining the guy-party? Why open your home to people if you can't even treat them right? The Messiah brings His chosen Twelve to your house and you just throw some pastrami on the table and sit down like *you're* the guest?"

Yes, Marthas, *yes.* Your house and your table you will always have. Our Lord is with us at appointed times. When He visits us, the better part is to be with Him no matter what the house looks like or what's prepped for lunch or who your company is. When Jesus offers Himself, the right answer is "Yes, Lord; I believe that You are the Christ, the Son of God, who is coming into the world" (John 11:27). If that is the right answer, the dishes can and *should* wait until after church.

They will still need to be washed. The disciples will still have to be fed. Stopping to receive what Jesus has to give often complicates the demands of the day. That is why He gives us the Sabbath. Without it, there is no chance for the Marthas of the world to remember that there is more to life than a well-kept house. The pressure to feed hungry people and beat back chaos for another day can feel overwhelming, and that is why there is a day on which God commands us to hang up the towel, sit down, listen, and be served.

Have you ever noticed what's going on when we sing, "Lord, now lettest Thou Thy servant depart in peace"? The dishes are getting washed. The Nunc Dimittis is sung while the pastor cleans up after the meal he served. The Divine Service is truly the most restful hour of a woman's week. It's the one time someone else hosts, and she is the honored guest who is invited to eat, drink, and be at peace. It's the answer to that prayer about catching a break; the realization of the fantasy where someone else does *all* the work while we kick back for once.

It's also probably not the answer we envisioned. The Divine Service is not a spa treatment; Holy Communion is not lunch out with the girls; the proclaimed Word of God is not an inspirational speech; the absolution of our sins is not the affirmation our flesh wants. That is not how God works. He wants us to be good, not comfortable. He feeds us what we need so that we will grow into a hunger for the things that will make us healthy and strong, rather than indulging our babyish tastes for whatever is soft and sweet. The house of God is an acquired taste for many people, but it begins with trust that what He offers us is what we need, and that His Word is true.

So, Marthas, take Him at that Word. The Church's hospitality queen is not Martha Stewart, but the repentant overachiever Martha of Bethany. It is not the end of the world for supper to be late. It is more important for little old you to receive the gifts of God than for all those people to have a perfect crown roast served out of a sparkling kitchen promptly at noon. The forgiveness of sins by Word and Sacrament is delivered at a time and place well away from the stove. It is characterized by gracious words you don't have to come up with, and cleaning and feeding you don't have to do. Turn off the lights. No one's going to see that mess, and it's important for the people who gather at the tables you set to see that you're an honored guest in the Lord's house too. One thing's needful, and it isn't a clean counter, but the clean heart only Jesus can create in each of us.

If We Confess Our Sins

Here are some sins:

Stealing

Gossip

Envy

Lust

Murder

Profanity

Greed

Ew, yuck. Let's clean this up some. Here are some fake sins:

Working too hard

Being a perfectionist

Not being able to forgive myself

Not taking time for me

Not realizing how beautiful I am

The second list is what we would like to believe are our sins. This doesn't mean that they can't be real things. Any strength can bloat itself out of its own benefits. But the fact that each of these things is nothing more than an overdone strength shows what they're really about. They are sneaky ways of complimenting ourselves. We are too good, too conscientious, too generous, and too caring.

We are too ridiculous. The favorite fake sins of Facebook are not the true spiritual dangers in our lives. Getting hung up on them is like donating to research for water intoxication instead of cancer. Drinking too much water can kill you, but it's hardly humanity's prevailing health threat. Concern over fake sins diverts our attention from the cancer in our souls. Someone who can't forgive herself for not painting that trim sleeps just fine after failing to pray for five months. A woman hung up on meta-analyzing her own beauty doesn't think twice about the ugly joke she made about her co-worker. The perfectionist only knows she is one compared to the unthankful slobs about whom she thinks hatefully while she puts away their shoes.

Fake sins make all kinds of sense. It's easy to cry on the world's shoulder about having heroically run oneself into the ground in the service of others. It's pretty awful to confess to a pastor in the stead of Christ that you're in the habit of bashing your in-laws behind their backs and loving the way it feels. The world will give you a big hug, tell you what a selfless person you are, and treat you to Starbucks. All a pastor has to offer is eternal redemption before God Almighty because of Jesus' innocent and atoning death.

First John 1:8 says, "If we say we have no sin, we deceive ourselves, and the truth is not in us." Crediting ourselves with fake sins is just a slimier way of doing this. It's a pretty big stretch to find *being too hard on myself* in the Ten Commandments. The Law shows our sin by telling us that every one of us is a short temptation away from hating another person and trying to take every good thing she has. Any sin a person has not committed is one for which she has lacked either opportunity or taste, and every sin will kill faith.

Most unbelievers are not kept from faith because they do not believe there is a God. What they do not believe in is their own sin. They think they're pretty good. They don't believe there is anything so wrong with them that they need forgiveness in any significant way, certainly not an eternal one. If there is a hell, it was only invented for Hitler, and what makes it so hellish is that he's there all alone.

But John goes on: "If we confess our sins, He is faithful and just to forgive us our sins and to cleanse us from all unrighteousness" (1 John 1:9). Forgiveness is not a self-improvement project for our personalities to help us like ourselves better and succeed. It is our only hope of finding favor with a holy God. This means that we must be honest about what our sins are. We have to look in the mirror of God's Law without makeup or Spanx. When we make a true confession of what we see there, we want and receive forgiveness in Jesus for what it is really worth.

THE SIXTH COMMANDMENT: NOT JUST FOR MEN!

Hello! What brings you here? Did you glance through the table of contents and think this essay might be more interesting than the others? Or are you reading through the book in an orderly fashion and you just arrived on this page? Either way, hello! Thanks for being here. Please read on.

We all know what the Sixth Commandment states, right? If not, flip to Exodus 20:14 or Deuteronomy 5:18: "You shall not commit adultery."

We all know how Rev. Dr. Martin Luther explained this commandment, right? If not, flip to the first section of Luther's Small Catechism. If you don't own Luther's Small Catechism, I highly recommend it! It's a great little book, and you won't regret the time or cost it takes to put it on your shelf, or better yet, put it in your head. But just to be sure we're all on the same page . . . "*What does this mean? We should fear and love God so that we lead a sexually pure and decent life in what we say and do, and husband and wife love and honor each other*" (Small Catechism, meaning of the Sixth Commandment).

Women's interpretation of the Sixth Commandment = "You shall not commit adultery. What does this mean? Men should stop checking out chicks and lusting and viewing

pornography and thinking impure thoughts and doing impure things with their bodies and this is a real struggle for
them."

Maybe you are someone who totally gets that *Numero
Seis* applies to you, in which case, I commend you. Unfortunately, there are plenty of godly gals who think this is a
man's problem more than a woman's.

The Sixth Commandment is not just for men! While
women may break it in ways that are different and seem-
ingly more benign, a broken commandment is a broken
commandment. It requires confession and absolution and
renewed resolve, by God's grace. We're going to take those
things in order here.

First, please check all that apply. (Mental checks, friends.
Mental checks. Not literal. This is not a *Cosmo* quiz and you
will not be awarded with a Bedroom Personality summa-
ry at the end of it. Then again, if you're holding your very
own copy of this book, you're free to do whatever you'd like
with it. But you can be sure my copy won't be marked up on
these pages.)

___ You take *Cosmo* quizzes to determine your Bedroom
Personality. (Ha-ha, kidding. No, but seriously.)

___ You read romance novels and sense sensations in
personal areas.

___ You use the bedroom as a dangling carrot to tease;

___ Or as leverage to get what you want.

___ You drink enough at a bar or club or office party or anywhere to make that random make-out mostly just funny.

___ You watch a racy movie, read a racy online article, hang a racy poster, make a racy joke, laugh at a racy joke, share racy pics of yourself, view racy pics of others, or think/say/do anything else involving the adjective *racy*.

___ You think about your professor in marriage-only ways.

___ You think about your ex-boyfriends in marriage-only ways.

___ You think about your current boyfriend in marriage-only ways.

(Let's speed things along here, shall we?)

___ You think about **anyone who isn't your husband** in marriage-only ways.

(There. That captures it.)

___ You act out any of those thoughts.

___ You scorn your husband's marital appetite.

___ You engage in what polite people used to call "solitary vice."

___ You are too tired or too headachy or unwilling-for-some-other-dodgy-reason to satisfy your husband's marital appetite.

___ You wish McDreamy or Jack Reacher or some other crush were your husband/boyfriend/make-out buddy.

___ You speak/think ill of marriage in general.

___ You speak/think ill of your husband in particular.

___ You struggle with homosexual thoughts/deeds.

___ You do not actually consider yourself a homosexual but nevertheless engage in same-sex contact that is marital in nature.

___ You chat online or on the phone or in person in a flirty or provocative way with someone who is not your husband.

___ You aim to seduce or at least catch someone's eye.

___ You have ever thought/said/done any of those things ever in your life.

Any check marks?
Even just one? One teensy-tiny one? Yeah. Me too. :(
The movies 50 *Shades of Grey* and *Magic Mike* grossed way too well at the box office. Harlequin novels dominate

the shelves at used-book stores. Sex-toy parties are a real thing, and they aren't always (or ever?) tasteful gatherings of wives with healthy, marital impulses who are respectful of their spouse's and their own bodies and dignity. The industry sectors that profit from women's Sixth Commandment issues are doing just fine, which means that all of us aren't.

And those "affairs of the heart," as women like to call them? Those are a big, bad deal too. Just because a woman might only feel *for* a man without actually feeling *him* does not mean that she is living chastely. Chastity has to do with one's whole self and is not limited to those sexual parts of it. Adultery can take place in a heart (Matthew 5:28) as easily as it can take place in a hotel room. In fact, it happens more easily in a heart because there's no one there to see the sin and cast judgment. A heart is the most convenient place for an affair because it is so rarely found out, unless it's acted upon. But a really good way to keep from acting on impure thoughts is to keep from thinking such thoughts in the first place.

All women, whether married or single, fail to lead perfectly chaste and decent lives. Just because our methods of breaking this commandment are sneakier doesn't make them less sinful. To wag our fingers at men is foolish and false.

When we get past pretending that this commandment is beneath our feminine dignity, we find ourselves holding the same end of the stick that the man is holding. It's the "poor, miserable sinner" end. Sexual sin is sin with an extra shot of haunting stigma. This category of sin feels worse and embarrasses more because it involves those parts of us that are private. Because it's all so private, we don't even like to think about it. And we definitely don't want to talk about it.

If that checklist made you feel like you were being accused of something, it did what it was supposed to do. God's Law accuses. That is one of its primary functions. Repentance first requires acknowledgment.

Good news, though—and by good news, I mean Gospel.

The Lord does not leave us in the blasted hot shame of those accusations ringing in our burning ears.

We are called to confess those shameful things. We have the sure promise that "He is faithful and just to forgive us our sins and to cleanse us from all unrighteousness" (1 John 1:9). All those impure thoughts, words, and deeds are completely forgiven by the One who was and is forever faithful, pure, and holy. We are disgraceful. He is grace-full.

When we have Christ's forgiveness, we get to live as one who has been made clean. Sexual sins (along with all others that are forgiven) should not torment a forgiven child of God. Christ's response to the woman caught in adultery goes for every one of us. It is a word of both pardon and power. After handily dismantling her accusers' ammunition, this exchange took place:

> Jesus stood up and said to her, "Woman, where are they? Has no one condemned you?" She said, "No one, Lord." And Jesus said, "Neither do I condemn you; go, and from now on sin no more." (John 8:10–11)

If that isn't a delicious gulp of Gospel, I don't know what is. First, that our Lord would look on our most humiliating sins with boundless mercy and grant full forgiveness. And second, that He would be so very good as to give us the strength to do better in those secret, sinful struggles, by His grace and with His help.

One more glug for good measure . . .

"Neither do I condemn you; go, and from now on sin no more."

Eight, Nine, Ten—Last, but Not Least

If you were asked to rank the Commandments in order of importance, numbers eight, nine, and ten might just keep their place at the bottom. Things like idolatry and murder are big no-nos. Adultery and theft are wrong, though maybe not as bad as shooting someone. But lying? Coveting? Come on. Lying is bad, but surely not on par with physical harm or putting other things before God. And most of us suspect that coveting might just be thrown in to make the number an even ten.

There may be something to those observations, and it's a bit artificial to rank something like the Commandments, but there's a strong case to be made for commandments eight, nine, and ten being every bit as harmful as the others.

God formed Adam out of the dust and placed him in the Garden of Eden. God made to spring up "every tree that is pleasant to the sight and good for food" (Genesis 2:9). In addition to the trees, there was water: a river runs through it. Then God made the animals, and last, He made Adam's gorgeous companion, Eve.

The grass is greener than green. What more could they want? There is certainly nothing they needed. Lunch is literally low-hanging fruit. There are no thorns or briers to disturb the evening stroll by the river. The temperature is perfect; no sweatshirt (or even shirt) required. They have nothing to fear from the animals.

Yet even in this setting—and here is the power of a lie—the serpent succeeds in making Eve dissatisfied with *Paradise*. She is not content with God's will for her in the place that God declared "very good."

The serpent is cunning. He is a master of exaggeration and persuasion. "Did God actually say, 'You shall not eat of any tree . . .'?" (Genesis 3:1). He twists God's Word. His half-truths and outright lies tempt Eve to place herself above God's decree. Dietrich Bonhoeffer, in his book *Creation and Fall*, describes this scene, where Eve sits in judgment of God's command.

With the snake's false testimony dancing in her head, she looks over at the tree and wonders if God is holding out on her. The food looks good. It is a delight to the eyes. Plus, the tree was to be desired to make one wise. What's not to like? So she takes some fruit and eats, and then she gives some to Adam.

That right there is the power of the lie and coveting: even Paradise cannot live up. *Nothing* can satisfy like a lie. The fantasy is not true and it never will be, and this is exactly what makes it seem better than real life ten times out of ten.

Coveting makes us unhappy with the reality of our life. It is an unquenchable thirst because it is a thirst for unreality. The grass looks greener on the other side and we totally don't get that it's AstroTurf or CGI or a mirage. It's pretend. It's false belief. All that make-believe drives to dissatisfaction and discontentment with the adequate yard that God's actually given us.

Fiction portrays idealistic scenarios that represent no one's actual life. The Follow-Your-Heart philosophy does not acknowledge the terrible damage in the wake of such a self-centered hunt. The Hollywood effect on us is often subtle. There are a bunch of characters doing what we all wish we could do. They can make it all happen without the hang-ups of real life. Their world is fantasy, but we foolishly think it can be our real deal.

We keep chasing after what's not ours no matter what dismal outcomes we've bumped into before. We convince ourselves that *this* time, this situation, is surely different. We know there are times when God's commands *really* apply, and that the commands *usually* protect us from something harmful, but we trick ourselves into thinking that *this* time is not one of them. *I would truly be happy if _____ were my situation in life.* Fill in that blank with something other than what God has given, whether it's another car, house, job, boss, income, spouse, child, parent, lifestyle, or whatever.

Lies and coveting lead us to imagine that a happy future is just behind Door Number 2 or whatever door isn't rightfully ours. We picture opening that door to our ideal life rather than to the death and grief that God tells us sin *will* bring about. As the proverb teaches, "There is a way that seems right to a man, but its end is the way to death" (Proverbs 14:12).

The way that seems right is a deception. It's a temptation like the one the serpent put to Eve: You can be like God. You can decide what is right and wrong for yourself. You can work your way out of this substandard chapter in your life and write your own happy ending.

Satan's lie led someone who was created in God's image and likeness to believe that she could somehow be *more* like God by disobeying Him. This is the madness of the sin of commandments eight, nine, and ten. That stripe of sin conditions us for the unreal, which can only come at the expense of the truth.

The apostle Paul shared a secret to counter the lie and the coveting: "I have learned in whatever situation I am to be content" (Philippians 4:11). Contentment responds to the temptations of the world, the devil, and our sinful nature: I don't need that lie. I don't need that imaginary life. I have everything I need and more right here with me in real life. "I can do all things through Him who strengthens me" (Philippians 4:13).

Contentment looks out *our own* front door and recognizes that the neighbor's lawn doesn't apply and isn't what's important. What really matters—what deserves our appreciation and our tending and our attention—is the grass that constitutes our rightful and God-given lot in life. In looking out at the garden, we must remind ourselves that the secret to happiness is not the lying whisper that the snake hisses in our ear. The secret is in the plain Word of God. There we find contentment in the one true God, who, "richly and daily provides me with all that I need to support this body and life" (from Luther's Small Catechism, explanation of the First Article of the Apostles' Creed).

ACTUALLY, GOD MIGHT GIVE YOU MORE THAN YOU CAN HANDLE

There are a lot of things the Bible doesn't say. For example, it doesn't say, "Cleanliness is next to godliness," for which we can all be thankful. It also doesn't say, "God helps those who help themselves." And another thing the Bible doesn't say is "God won't give you more than you can handle."

What do people and refrigerator magnets mean when they say, "God won't give you more than you can handle"?

> That if one is given more than one can handle, one vaporizes, explodes, vanishes, or otherwise ceases to exist?

> That one's trials are precise measurements of one's capacity for handling (for example: God only allows people who can handle being mugged to be mugged)?

> That if one fails to handle something, one is on the receiving end of divine incompetence?

> That anything a person has not experienced is something God knows to be beyond that person's capacity for handling?

That this is just another one of those times when no one can really help you with what you're going through, but well-meaning people will make useless comments anyway?

This popular statement is perhaps a paraphrase of 1 Corinthians 10:13, which says, "No temptation has overtaken you that is not common to man. God is faithful, and He will not let you be tempted beyond your ability, but with the temptation He will also provide the way of escape, that you may be able to endure it." The verse is not about life situations but about temptation to sin. Even more troubling, it says that we *are*, with God's help, able to resist temptation and avoid sin, although we know we are sinners by nature.

All of this is another way of saying that our ways are not God's ways. When we face problems, we want friends to sympathize, therapists to hear us out and help us move on, and a cheerleading squad to tell us that the way we're dealing with everything is absolutely R-I-G-H-T! But none of those are what God primarily wants for us. All of life's problems are symptoms of our greatest and truest problem: sin. Our problems are caused by sin, and they tempt us to sin. In particular, problems entice us to blame others, shirk our responsibilities, and doubt the goodness of God. They are a prime opportunity for self-excuse, self-pity, and self-absorption.

Those temptations are what God wants us to escape. He has *not* promised not to give us more than we can handle, as anyone who has lived through a tragedy knows. There isn't a person on this earth who imagines a scenario like being assaulted, losing one's livelihood, losing a beloved person, or contracting a disease and thinks, "Yeah, I'd do pretty well with that." Those who "handle" such things are the ones who trust that He who spared not His own Son seeks what is best for us. Even though He appoints crosses for each of us to bear, the way of escape God has provided is Himself. He forgives the doubt, anger, fear, and despair that arise in our sinful hearts in response to trouble. He lived the problem-filled life of sinners not so that we wouldn't have problems, but so we would see that there is such a thing as a faithful life in a fallen world.

Often people seek to comfort the suffering with unhelpful words, and "God won't give you more than you can handle" is surely at the top of those pseudo-biblical platitudes. But Scripture is full of people who demonstrate faith's real answer to hardship:

Job responds to losing all his possessions and his ten children by saying, "Naked I came from my mother's womb, and naked shall I return. The Lord gave, and the Lord has taken away; blessed be the name of the Lord" (Job 1:21). When this group of life-size sucker punches is followed up with a bout of festering sores, his wife advises him to curse God. He asks her, "Shall we receive good from God, and shall we not receive evil?" (Job 2:10).

Martha, mourning the death of her brother, is asked by Jesus if she believes that He is the resurrection and the life, and that those who believe in Him will never die. Only four days after burying her beloved Lazarus, she answers, "Yes, Lord; I believe that You are the Christ, the Son of God, who is coming into the world" (John 11:27).

Anna was widowed after just seven years of marriage.

As a result, "She did not depart from the temple, worshiping with fasting and prayer night and day" (Luke 2:37).

Martha didn't take the loss of her brother as evidence that Jesus was a fraud. Anna didn't allow her husband's death to become a reason for avoiding the house of God. Job acknowledged unreservedly that his suffering had come from God, and he still looked forward with awe to seeing his Redeemer in the flesh. None of these people were happy about what had happened to them; they didn't feel pain or grief any less than others do. But they *believed* that God was good. They trusted His promise to make all things new. They believed they were sinners who saw through a glass darkly, and that God's ways were higher than their own. They believed there was more to life than this life, and that the life to come was much more important.

If these heroes of the faith are no different than we are, neither are their trials different than ours. We may suffer, and horribly. God may give us more than we can handle physically, emotionally, or intellectually. But the crosses Jesus told us we would bear do not amount to a personal resilience contest. He tells us forthrightly, "In the world you will have tribulation. But take heart; I have overcome the world" (John 16:33b). Our suffering is God's personal call to repentance, trust, and hope. He has provided the way of escape through His own life, death, and resurrection, and He has endured every temptation we face. He sympathizes with us in our weakness, He hears our prayers, and He absolves us of every sin we confess, including those occasioned by suffering. To believe this is to "handle" whatever life hands us.

Sophia, Sophronia, and Babylon

Modesty is the down-to-earth sister of humility. Being modest means not drawing unnecessary attention to oneself or extracting praise from others. This should be as easy as it sounds, but since we all know it isn't, here we go.

We'll take the reasons for modesty from least significant to most. First, it is tacky not to be modest. Immodesty shows poor taste. The main thing it puts on display is one's own arrogance. It is cutting in line, taking the biggest doughnut, and one-upping someone else's story. The small gain of such actions is beggared by the damage they do to one's reputation. Everyone waits so eagerly for the known one-upper to one-up that they never hear what she says. She becomes infamous only for her one-upmanship. Immodesty fails to take into account that one's self-assessment might be embarrassingly wrong. It is often disingenuous; how else could a whole nation full of women crippled with low self-esteem constantly be buying bikinis? Haven't we all seen a poorly selected bikini or two?

The next problem with immodesty is that it is likely to occasion sin in others, particularly envy and coveting. Coveting is the coveter's problem. But only a facile and self-serving approach to Christian life allows a total disregard of the Christian lives of others. Blowing off another Christian's struggle, sneering at it, or abandoning her to it is unkind and unloving. Dressing immodestly is cut from the same cloth as porking down a footlong in front of someone who is trying to lose weight or letting one's gorgeous vibrato take over "Happy Birthday." It's not how considerate people act. A person can be just as happy eating her footlong when her dieting friend isn't around, and the dieter won't have been forced into unnecessary footlonging. Immodesty is thinking and reasoning like a child, or pretending to, which is worse. We can't stop other people from sinning, and we can't know exactly what sets them off, which is why neighborliness ranks lower among the reasons to be modest. But it is willfully ignorant to argue that other people shouldn't be considered in assessing one's own modesty. Putting an ignoble pleasure before a fellow believer's fight with sin is selfish and cruel.

On to the next crisis of modesty. In calling the attention of others to the self, the self demands its own attention and investment. Higher heights of attention-earning must be reached. New accessories are required, constant expenditures must be made, and time must be spent in front of the mirror to make sure the desired effect is being achieved. *Is this mega-houndstooth thing a good idea? Is $130 too much for a facial cream? Mommy is still doing her hair; start another Yo Gabba Gabba!* St. Jerome lamented in the fourth century, "Today you may see women cramming their wardrobes with dresses, changing their gowns from day to day . . . while Christ[26] lies at the door naked and dying."[27] Women those days! Then again, perhaps we ourselves have some

---

26 Ah, there He is. All readers whose brains have begun rumbling about the need for a Gospel-oriented conversation about modesty are encouraged to go ahead and have one.

27 Quoted in *Treasury of Daily Prayer* (St. Louis: Concordia, 2009), 770.

experience with overstuffed wardrobes. Immodesty disables charity because it prioritizes the self. The more I spend on lipstick, the less I have to give to a person who would eat a lipstick if she had one. Immodesty is, ironically, nothing to be proud of.

The greatest trouble with immodesty is its previously mentioned relationship to humility. There is only one reason to draw attention to oneself: attention feeds pride, the first and worst sin. It likes being looked at. It wants the esteem of men. Immodesty is ignoring how Jesus told us flat out that whoever exalts himself will be humbled, and what that means for choosing seats at suppertime. As the biggest reason to be modest, pride needs the least explanation. Running from pride is the first lesson from Christian Life 101.

The call to modesty means doing one's best to look nice in a humble way. For most of us, that will mean being the person whom no one identifies as the belle of the ball but is remembered later as having been kind and gracious and actually looking quite nice, now that one thinks of it. The truly beautiful can't help being noticed, but there's a tax on that too. A beautiful woman forgoes certain benefits to gain the benefits of modesty. It's one thing to be beheld, and another to be ogled. It is a blessed mercy that the subject of these verbs is not totally powerless to affect which one applies more to her. Moreover, beauty is fleeting (Proverbs 31:30), which is why it's a bad idea for anyone to have too much invested in her own appearance. Belle today, battle-ax tomorrow.

Exodus lets us know that man-eating is out for the Christian lady, but the Book of Proverbs gets more personal. Big chunks of the early chapters are spent warning young men to steer clear of girls who didn't like what Exodus had to say and advising them instead to seek out a grand lady named Wisdom (*Sophia* in Greek). Sophia with her house and her seven pillars is pretty intimidating. She probably feels as irrelevant to the average female as the beauty most of us don't have in any serious way (pretty girls: we know it's not your fault). Sophia is the Church. She is our true mother, our guide through life, and the image of the perfect beauty God will give each of us at the end of all things. But for every day and while we work on getting wiser, any of us can be a highly effective *Sophronia* (prudence). We might imagine her as Sophia's practical friend, who makes sure everyone has a coaster and is totally fine with being seen in galoshes. Sophronia isn't the homecoming queen or the valedictorian, but she's more than able to take care of business, act decent, and get her hair in order without much warning. She's a nice Christian lady each of us can be in our own way.

Whether we relate more to glorious Sophia or good-natured Sophronia, we would do well to observe that neither of those ladies looks one bit like Proverbs' lady Folly, who shows up in Revelation as Babylon the Great. They do not take fashion tips from her or try to imitate her style. Babylon is a prostitute, a porn star, a swarming sack of everything disgusting. She is the one who disposed of *beauty* as a metric for female appearance and replaced it with *sexy* and *hot*. It is the duty of men to look away from her in obedience so that they might one day look away in revulsion. It is the duty of women, though their greatest desire is to be looked on with desire, to refuse to imitate her no matter how badly men fail in their duty. There is no accounting for taste, but there is such a thing as bad taste. We who live in a tasteless land must deliberately teach ourselves good taste and work to be the kind of woman God would have His daughters be. Only a fool falls for foxy Babylon, whether that means hiring her or becoming her.

But we don't have to get all philosophical about it either. St. Cyril of Jerusalem was blowing minds way back in the fourth century *(women those days!)* with this piece of advice: "Rather let your clothing be simple: it is not for ornamentation but for the necessity of covering, not so that you can become vain but so that you can keep warm in winter and cover the nakedness of your body."[28] Now *there's* a modest treatment of modesty. If you're so vain you think this essay was about you . . . maybe you're right?

---

28 St. Cyril of Jerusalem, Catechesis IV.29 (Migne vol. 33, translation by Heath R. Curtis).

Being Special Is Special!

First, the good news: everyone IS special. The preschool teachers of the world have that right.

The bad news is that everyone has decided to be jerks about it. No statement can be made without someone getting terribly hurt over its exclusion of her particular situation. She's not married (or she is), so this article doesn't apply. She has kids (or she doesn't), so this bit of conventional wisdom is a mean thing to say. She didn't go to college (or she did), so this recommendation is insensitive. Her kid has special needs (or doesn't), so this Internet meme is presumptuous. She has an illness (or she heard that a lot of people do), so this doctrine of the Church is discriminatory. We have all become specialists in finding reason to take offense.

The truth is that since we are all special, we have all felt excluded at some time. There will always be someone who knows better than you why your adult child has become a Mormon, or how to get your husband to church, or what you should do about the divorce that's ripping apart your family, or how your mother-in-law should be cared for, or what you should be doing with the daylight hours, or how your neuro-atypical child should be raised, or why your child is neuro-atypical, or how many kids you should have, or how you should go about acquiring the kids you don't have, or why your marriage isn't what you thought it would be, or why you're not married, or whatever your personal situation of heightened sensitivity is. That's one thing about us that isn't special. We've all been hurt by someone else's opinion of the way we handle things.

At the same time, it would be childish to imagine that situations of offense are entirely out of our control. Conflict grows in two directions. Someone who tries to be careful about giving offense can be far less guarded in her willingness to take it. Another person's soapbox becomes our stumbling block, and it's likely that the soapbox is about little more than soap. Someone else's basically inconsequential ideas about a laundry surfactant or a diet or a magazine become our grounds for despising a sister in Christ. *She doesn't know what it's like for me, she's giving other people bad ideas, or she's just plain stupid.* Who's the special snowflake here? The person who finds some joy in sharing the silly things that mean something to her in this silly life, or the person who can't abide any difference in taste or opinion?

But even when it comes to serious topics, we would do well to consider carefully our high view of ourselves. Identifying ourselves as exceptional is much easier than seeing that we are exactly as subject to human haplessness as everyone else. We all experience complications, rottenness, and exclusion as a matter of course. G. K. Chesterton writes in *The Uses of Diversity*, "If it comes to claiming exceptional treatment, the very people who will claim it will be those who least deserve it. . . . The men who really think themselves extraordinary are the most ordinary rotters on earth." There is such a thing as being exceptional, but if it were as common as the sum of our diagnoses, there wouldn't be. Each of us has crosses to bear. The Christian life is about bearing one another's burdens, not trying to get every available pair of shoulders under *our* burdens. Our own hardships are where we gain sympathy for the pains of others and the knowledge necessary to help them.

Whereas being quick to anger is less special than ever, it creates the opportunity for a different specialization. We could opt out of the culture of offendedness. The Christian woman could respond with grace at those times when she feels excluded (and certainly at those times when she is merely annoyed). Maybe she could smile about it or decide not to make a sharp comment. Sometimes she might be able to get a laugh out of how weirdly different the world's people are; sometimes she might need to cry on the shoulder of a true friend. She could recognize the pain she has felt during times of exclusion as an opportunity to cultivate her own sensitivity to the struggles of others. She could exercise that most Christian virtue, humility, and be ruled not by a pang of emotion, but by the word of Christ: "Blessed are the peacemakers" (Matthew 5:9).

Feeling hurt is not always a choice we get to make, but we do get to decide how we react to it. A lot of effort goes into teaching children not to call names, hit, or pitch fits when things don't go their way. Grownuphood is when we work to perfect that discipline, not when we escape it. It would be a shame for all the work our preschool teachers did to go to waste.

On a Search for Self

When reading Scripture, one should always search for Christ. A pastor said that Jesus could be found on every single page of the Bible. Probably a lot of pastors said that, actually, because it's true and it's important. Christ is the key to understanding the Word.

A more common approach to studying Scripture, though, and especially among women, is to search for one's self on the pages. This is not all bad. It is good to connect God's Word to our daily lives. As we study how God worked out His plan for salvation, we want to know not only that it is all true in the factual sense but also that it is all true *for us*, in the personal sense. Seeing ourselves in the salvation narrative is a very good thing.

Sometimes, though, when our sinful nature does the steering, we find ourselves in all the wrong places. For the purpose of this essay, we will use the Book of Proverbs as an example.

Here we go. We are embarking on a journey through Proverbs, and while we know we should be looking for Christ first and foremost, we are going to indulge in a little distraction and look for ourselves. *Oh self . . . where are you? Ready or not, here I come!*

Proverbs 5:3: "For the lips of a forbidden woman drip honey, and her speech is smoother than oil." That really reminds me of Heidi. The way she talks to men is awful. Just the other day, I saw her sidling up to a guy again and he totally didn't even understand that she had an agenda. I can't stand how many guys fall for her; she is not worth their time. Those guys should read this verse, I guess, just so they would get what she's up to. Sneaky forbidden woman with her terrible beguiling and her plunging necklines. There's a reason we're not friends.

Proverbs 9:13: "The woman Folly is loud; she is seductive and knows nothing." This passage is some kind of fancy metaphor, but it actually reminds me of that real lady I was standing behind yesterday at the grocery store. She was way too loud and none of her blathering was even worth saying. What a ditz. If I were going to say such stupid things, I'd at least say them quietly so not everyone would be subjected to my foolishness.

Proverbs 11:22: "Like a gold ring in a pig's snout is a beautiful woman without discretion." So true! So very true! I have talked to my friend Kayla about this a million times and I cannot get through to her. I've said, "You have to think about what you're doing. You won't always have that shiny hair to flip and those long lashes to bat when you need to get out of a jam." She never learns, though! Being discreet shouldn't be that impossibly hard, but for some reason it eludes her. I guess I'll just have to keep helping her as best I can. This passage reminds me how important it is.

Proverbs 12:4: "An excellent wife is the crown of her husband, but she who brings shame is like rottenness in his bones." The crown of her husband . . . hmmm . . . I guess I've never thought of myself that way before, but it does make sense! So glad I don't bring shame. Rotten bones sound gross, and probably painful too.

Proverbs 19:13: "A wife's quarreling is a continual dripping of rain."

Proverbs 21:19: "It is better to live in a desert land than with a quarrelsome and fretful woman." Poor Mr. Anderson. From the continual dripping of rain to a desert land—either way, he's got it bad! Do those two ever stop fighting? His wife is constantly nagging and freaking out about something. She needs to learn to relax a little and not worry so much. Like, how many panic attacks did she have in the last month alone? Her husband is probably desperate for a break from her fussing.

Proverbs 25:24: "It is better to live in a corner of the housetop than in a house shared with a quarrelsome wife." Ditto. More about Mrs. Anderson. And actually, Mrs. Smith too, now that I think about it. What's wrong with wives these days?

Proverbs 30:20: "This is the way of an adulteress: she eats and wipes her mouth and says, 'I have done no wrong.'" DisGUSting. Can't even think about that. Way too nasty. Doesn't apply here, so moving on.

Proverbs 31:10–31: Yes!! There's so much good stuff in this passage. I love it! I could study this every day! An excellent wife is hard to find. I would agree with that. I'm probably one of the few who really fits this description in a lot of ways. Now, I will admit that I don't get it all right because I am a sinner . . . but looking at that list, I'm not far off! Husband trusts me? Check. I do him good and not harm? Check. I don't know about all the wool and flax and ships business, but I do work way harder than just about any other woman

I know. It's definitely still dark when I get up, at least in the winter for sure. I make the meals for everybody and I take care of the laundry. Verse 17 is definitely me. I make it to my kettle bells class four times a week. Etc. Etc. Etc. Skipping ahead a bit, "Many women have done excellently, but you surpass them all" (v. 29). Yes, Self, that sums you up nicely!

And just like that, the Search for Self in the Book of Proverbs comes to a very satisfying conclusion. Unfortunately, it was an arrogant, delusional, and unfaithful handling of the text.

All of this has been overstated, but there is some truth in it, which is why it stings. When the Law should be functioning as a mirror to show us our sin, we look into the glass and see the face of our neighbor who is constantly failing. When the Law should be functioning as a curb and a guide to show us the boundaries and the right way, we are convinced we're already on track and we don't really have all that much room for improvement.

As we read Scripture, we must see ourselves as the sinners. Those sinner passages aren't just about someone else. They're about us! *We* need a Savior! *We* are the unfaithful, foolish, quarrelsome, shameful Bride with deceitful charm and vain beauty. When we understand this, we will keep our eyes peeled for the Savior because we will know how very desperately we need Him. Our Lord is the only perfect spouse. He is never given to infidelity, quarreling, contention, indiscretion, or folly. He is the way of Wisdom, unto life everlasting. When we see ourselves as the sinners and we search for Jesus, we find Him right where He has always promised to be, in the Word and in the Sacraments, offering forgiveness of sins, life, and salvation! *For us*, because we need it!

Romans 12:15—Vicarious Rejoicing with a Whole Heart

In Romans 12:15, we're called to rejoice with those who rejoice and mourn with those who mourn. Mourning with those who mourn sounds difficult, but it is actually a remarkable strength of women. Even women who do not consider themselves to be particularly sensitive or touchy-feely are likely to be moved when another is hurting in some way. It could be a family member or friend. It could be a complete stranger. It could be a puppy dog, for that matter. The point is, when a woman sees suffering or hears about it, her heart is nearly always moved to love and compassion.

It doesn't mean that we always have exactly the right words to say, but there is something inside of us that instinctively mourns with those who mourn. Prayer request time at a women's Bible study is one place where this becomes obvious. A story about a person going through a difficult time (could be a cousin of a neighbor of a lady's great-aunt's college roommate) nearly always gathers a collective and sincere sigh of sorrow from the group.

This side of the Romans 12:15 exhortation we have grasped pretty well, and without any intentional effort on our part. When we hear of another's pain or sorrow, we naturally want to give a hug or cobble together some words of heartfelt sympathy or say a prayer or make a casserole. We do those things almost without realizing we're doing them. This is a good gift. We thank God for this ability and tendency.

There is an interesting phenomenon, though, with respect to the first part of the verse. It would seem that the rejoicing appeal should be the easy one. Who doesn't like to rejoice? Yet, what often happens is that women do not rejoice genuinely or well with other women. Certainly, there are times when we hear a bit of good news and we're in party mode without difficulty. That is good! But it's not always that easy.

Someone gets a promotion. Someone runs a marathon. Someone buys a new home. Someone shows up looking awesome. Someone's kid wins a big scholarship. Someone's dad is elected mayor. Are we happy? Somewhat. It's hard to rejoice properly and sincerely, though, when our happiness is lodged under layers of jealousy, resentment, and a big comparison act on our part that finds our own achievements and joys lacking.

When we find out that our friend earned a chair in the horn section of the New York Philharmonic, her talent and hard work make us feel inadequate. *Well, shoot, what have I ever done?* Instead of rejoicing wholeheartedly, a part of our heart is busy making us feel like a chump.

When we find out that our friend is going on a cruise for free with her college bestie, her great opportunity makes us stew that good things never come our way and our life seems very ho-hum and tedious by comparison. *When will I get a break and a tan?* Instead of rejoicing wholeheartedly, a part of our heart is on the beach, where we wish the rest of us were.

When our friend shows up in a lovely, composed outfit complete with styled hair and tasteful makeup, we wish she didn't. If we're sitting around in yoga pants and a T-shirt and last night's wilted ponytail, everyone should! Instead of rejoicing wholeheartedly, a part of our heart is rotting with resentment and finding blame with a party who doesn't deserve it.

With prayers for an increase in all the relevant fruit described in Galatians 5, may the Lord grant that vicarious joy come to us more spontaneously and sincerely. Wouldn't it be something if we could rejoice as empathetically as we mourn? Fellow females could delight in knowing how genuinely we are cheering for them and with them. We can thank God for their blessings instead of analyzing and begrudging how they relate to ours. Rejoicing is actually really fun, especially when it's done with a whole heart!

Mirror, Mirror

Ephesians 5:29 states, "No one has ever hated his own flesh." Maybe no one has ever hated *his* own flesh, but I know plenty who have hated *her* own flesh.[29]

Women teeter on a narrow wire of self-regard. They are pulled in one of two directions, and sometimes both at once, which generates all kinds of confusing dissonance.

On one side is the woman who looks in the mirror and is repulsed. Everything is wrong. "Mirror, mirror, on the wall, who is the ugliest of them all?" Her conviction: "I am." From her face to her feet and every other inch of figure in between, this woman has no appreciation whatsoever for the hopeless mess that is her body.

Self-loathing and self-injuring are contrary to God's Word and will. When Scripture says that flesh is not for hating, it's stating the obvious, natural truth. The body is the temple of the Holy Spirit (1 Corinthians 6:19–20). To smack-talk or trash the joint is definitely not okay.

Further, when someone hates her body, she would do well to recall that this pretty much amounts to thinking ill of her Maker. If a statue's facial features aren't symmetrical, or if it is dimpled in the wrong cheek department, or if it's

---

29 Obviously, and sadly, there are also men who hate their flesh, but the focus of this book in general and this essay in particular is on women.

too tall or too short or too fat or too thin, or if it has cankles, or if its eyes are too squinty or its hair too fine or its pores too big or its teeth too yellow or its eyebrows too bushy or its chins too plentiful—those are all things for which the sculptor will be critiqued.

When a Christian woman is critical of her own flesh, she holds her Creator in contempt. Our heavenly Father knit us together in the womb. He did not do a bad job. We are "fearfully and wonderfully made" (Psalm 139:14). That goes for everyone, including the one who thinks she's the ugliest of them all.

On the other side is the woman who looks in the mirror and is enchanted. "Mirror, mirror, on the wall, who is the fairest of them all?" Her conviction: "I am." She devotes tremendous resources of energy, money, time, and willpower to the infatuated maintenance of her knockout self. Even in this camp, though, doubt creeps in. The perfect, *perfect* look is always one more eyebrow tweeze or one more sit-up or one more hair treatment away.

In both camps, self-absorption and too much time in front of the mirror perpetuate the prevailing problem. Hating your looks and idolizing your looks are two sides of the same coin. They are both vain and they are both far too concerned with the esteem of men.

Long before any magazine told us what was *en vogue*, the Lord had a plan for us that had nothing to do with our sense of fashion or our look. "For we are His workmanship, created in Christ Jesus for good works" (Ephesians 2:10). "You are not your own, for you were bought with a price. So glorify God in your body" (1 Corinthians 6:19b–20).

He made you. If you look in the mirror and think that you are wonderful, remember this is to His credit, not yours. If you look in the mirror and think that you're not wonderful, well, think again—because He said you are and He would know. Then let that be enough. We Christians are different. We Christians don't determine our worth or the worth of others based on cosmetic (which is to say: superficial) counter gobbledygook. "For the Lord sees not as man sees: man looks on the outward appearance, but the Lord looks on the heart" (1 Samuel 16:7).

Dear Sisters

You don't choose your family. You're born into it. The other members of the family are your relatives whether or not you have much in common with them beyond the bundle of genes that brought you together. Your personality will click with some and clash with others, but none of this changes the fact that family is family and will remain so regardless of how anyone feels about it. Friendships come and go, but your siblings, parents, grandparents, aunts, uncles, cousins, and children are all permanently positioned in that unchanging category of family.

Familial estrangement is very, very sad. Where there is a mother who will not speak to her daughter, a niece who mocks her aunt, or a grandmother who has no kind words for her granddaughter, there is tremendous heartache. The entire family feels it. Neutral members feel the feuding parties' pain in their own hearts too.

Dear sisters in the Lord, please understand that we in the Church are family. We share an eternal tie through Holy Baptism. We understand that we are children of God, but we often forget that makes us siblings to one another. We're joint heirs. We did not choose this family. This family is God's elect. God chose you for this family; God chose me and all the other members as well. Through water and the Word, you are my sisters and I am yours.

Dear sisters, I am sorry to say that I will sin against you. I will make you wish I wasn't in your family. I will hurt your feelings. I will tell your secret and betray your trust. I will be annoying, insensitive, and unloving. I will be forgetful and I'll miss your birthday. I will be selfish and expect a lot from you without giving much in return. I won't ask how your day is going because I will be too busy talking about mine. I will show favoritism to someone who isn't you. I will tell you that your idea is bad and I have a better one. I will be sarcastic, rude, and loud. I will lie to you. I will hurt your reputation to improve mine. I will make you wonder how we are even related; that is how terribly I will fail you. Without knowing precisely how or when these things will happen, I know that they will because I am a poor miserable sinner. This is not an excuse. It is a confession.

We say it together in church every Sunday. The whole family says it out loud, in fact, so we know we're all on the same page. These failings shouldn't surprise us. And yet it can feel impossibly hard to bear with one another's sins.

Dear sisters, please forgive me. Please forgive me when I ask for forgiveness. Please forgive me even when I don't ask for forgiveness. Please forgive me for my sake and for your sake and for the sake of the whole family.

Estrangement in the family of God is very, very sad. It is felt by all of the members. You might think the problem is just between you and one other, but the entire family will feel the strain. That's just how family works. When two people are not rightly related, everyone feels it and everyone hurts.

When a member of the family leaves one church to go to another because of a broken relationship, she has found a new house, but she hasn't actually joined a new family. Wherever we go, we're still members of the same family that we've all shared from the moment of our baptismal birth. When we commune at the Lord's Table, we do so not just with those under our roof. We commune with the entire family throughout all of Christendom.

That sinner in your family who seems impossible to love is also a saint. She is a saint because she is a person for whom Christ willingly shed His precious blood. Christ found it in His heart to love her. Jesus didn't wait for her to get it right or try harder or even say she was sorry. He loved her while she was still dead in sin, still spitting in His face, still shouting, "Crucify Him." He loved her while there was not one lovable thing about her. That goes for all of us. Not a single one of us had a single redeeming quality when He took it upon Himself to redeem us.

We in the family are called to love as Christ loved. We are called to forgive as Christ forgives. The saint side in each of us has to engage to handle the sinner side in every other member of the family. Though it is hard, we are all capable of this because we are joined with Christ. His mercy becomes our mercy. His grace, our grace. As we go about forgiving others, we also blessedly find ourselves on the forgiven end, both by Christ and by one another, our siblings in Him.

These spiritual siblings here below will remain our family members forever. Our Lord is preparing a dwelling place and a banquet for us to enjoy together with Him. To be estranged from any member of the family of God here on earth is to fail to repair and nurture an enduring relationship that is ours for all of time.

Selfies—Oh, Snap!

Computer spell check doesn't recognize the word *selfie* yet, but in about five years, it probably will. It was the Oxford Dictionaries Word of the Year in 2013.[30] The movement is gaining popularity, especially among younger generations, and *especially* among females. Autophotography is not inherently wrong. But anytime our sinful selfies are involved, there's a pretty good chance it's not a perfect practice.

Many women are self-conscious. This is why sisters or college roommates or BFFs so often ask one another, "How do I look?" We hope for assurances and compliments, but we are also receptive to correction such as "Your tag is sticking out," or "You have parsley in your teeth," or "My purple sweater might look better with those jeans, which, by the way, are fabulous."

With the dawn of selfies, though, we don't have to ask someone else to tell us how we look. We can take a picture of ourselves and decide if it makes the cut. *Snap!* It's that fast, and it's that easy. If we're not happy, we can take another, and another, and another. We can keep taking pictures until we are satisfied that we have captured the best possible version of ourselves. Then we delete all those

---

30   http://blog.oxforddictionaries.com/2013/11/word-of-the-year-2013-winner/ (accessed 1/1/15).

that weren't worth keeping. It's not so much that we want to know what we look like. It's more that we want to know what we look like when we're looking exactly as we want to look.

We work every angle. We can manipulate the lighting to ease the appearance of fine lines. If dark circles have us down, maybe the black and white setting will take the edge off. We don't need to be models to be airbrushed anymore. We can edit out our own skin blemishes and brighten up our own skin tone.

We can keep combing our bangs until they're sitting perfectly. Maybe that lip color is good but a bit too much, so blot once or twice until it's just right. As all of this primping goes on, no one is waiting for us and thinking we're ridiculous. We would feel silly asking someone else to take thirty-eight pictures of us, but when we're by ourselves, we don't feel silly at all.

Once the perfect look is achieved, it's time to post that winning shot to our social media outlet of choice. Done! No, not actually done. Now it's time to wait for the compliments to roll in. This is the equivalent of our roommate saying, "You look great!" but we have to hear it from one hundred–plus people to be satisfied. The refresh browser button won't rest until we've been adequately affirmed.

The following issues may not affect all selfie-takers but are nevertheless worthy of consideration.

Issue #1. The selfies way of life may be symptomatic of a woman's desire to be in control. Many women like to be behind the metaphorical wheel. This is a way to be behind and also in front of the actual button. I don't want to risk someone else messing up the photo. She probably wouldn't understand which ear is my favorite, after all. Or nostril. Or eyebrow. But by taking the picture myself, I can control which of all of those things are featured in the photo. I can have a picture taken *right* because I can do it myself. Uh oh—someone's full of her self-ie!

Issue #2. The selfies way of life may fan and fuel a person's insecurities. I don't want any of my imperfections to be seen. I obsess over my self-perceived flaws and hate to think that they might be on display for others. That tooth out of line on the bottom row? I can hide that if I set my smile just so. Oh good. Now no one will see that the tooth is kind of misaligned.

These concerns are usually quite trivial, but we will never believe that. If someone said, "I would never in a million years notice that tooth," we are sure there must be something wrong with that person. How could they *not* see that tooth? So the taking of selfies creates an even greater level of obsession. Now we're sniffing out our own flaws like a bloodhound, and we're finding far more than anyone else ever would. It's not really all that helpful, if you think about it.

Issue #3. The selfies way of life may remove a person from real, meaningful community. When we take photos of ourselves, we are nearly always by ourselves. Sure, there's an occasional selfie group shot, but quite often the Selfie Taker is the only subject on display and the only person in the room. Where a photo used to involve more than one person, it no longer does. There's no one else there now where we used to ask a real-life human being, "How do I look?" A blessing of community is that we are strengthened by others' praises and also by others' criticisms. Maybe that shirt isn't our best, but without our roommate there to say so, we'll never know.

The Selfies Life is one in which we become our own judge and our own standard-setter. We think we know best. We also contribute to the growth of our own insecurities because even when all the Likes roll in, we sadly think to ourselves, "If they'd seen the first thirty-seven attempts, they wouldn't have been so impressed." But since we're all alone with our Selfie selves, no one says what we would most like to hear: "No, really! You look great even without the Enhance button!"

The very best is when someone loves the unstaged, unedited version of us. Too bad that version is harder to find these days.

WHAC-A-MOLE

Have you ever played "Whac-A-Mole"? It's an arcade game with blinking lights and dinging noises. A little mole sticks his head through a hole and you whack it with a mallet. It retreats while other moles pop their heads through other holes. Eventually, the game powers down and the moles are gone. It's fun for a while, but it wouldn't be fun forever. Eventually, you are glad to walk away from those crazy moles.

Daily tasks keep popping up in life. You can sit down at your desk and reply to every e-mail and get all caught up. But by the time you return to your desk with your cup of coffee, there's another e-mail, isn't there? The little sticker on your windshield reminds you that your oil may be fine now, but it will need to be changed again before long. The buzzer on your dryer may be about to sound, indicating that your last load of laundry is done, but your hamper is only going to start filling again.

Brush your teeth; then brush them again. Plan and prepare a meal; then plan and prepare another. Make your bed; then make it again. Mow the lawn; then mow it again. Pay the bills; then pay them again. Clock out and spend a handful of hours somewhere else; then clock in again. Wipe a little person's nose . . . or something else . . . then wipe it again.

The relentless moles of life don't power down. The lights keep blinking and the dings keep dinging and the moles keep popping up. There is this constant, overwhelming feeling of "can't get it done, can't get ahead, can't get a break." We want to put down our mallet because our eyes are tired of watching for moles and our arm is tired of whacking away at them and our brain is tired of having to direct the eyes and arms to complete these tasks. We want to walk away from the moles, but we can't. If we walk away from them, they'll keep burrowing and burrowing, and there will be a bigger mess when we finally come back to them.

Think how I feel! I write a period and then I lumber on to the next sentence, which is just going to need another period.

Anyway, the point is (and we should be arriving there soon if we want this piece to have a final punctuation mark): this constitutes life.

Our lungs fill with air and then they refill. That's their job. They don't get a break, and we wouldn't want them to. We finish digesting one meal and our body needs another, so it sends more hungry signals. This constant feeling of un-done-ness is actually a sign of life. Our heart finishes one beat and moves on to the next. Please, dear heart, do not take a break, at least not a very long one, or I will be dead.

We complete a task and then move on to the next because we have a life to live. We check one thing off the to-do list. Along comes another to take its place. This can lead to despair: "I'll never be done." Or it can lead to joy: "I'll never be done!" There will always be something for us to do. This is what gives us a sense of purpose in the life the Lord has given us. It puts a value on our work. It emphasizes the importance of our particular callings in life.

If the e-mails stopped coming, we'd be out of a job. If the car never needed an oil change, it would mean we never took a trip. If the laundry hamper never refilled, uh . . . well, that would be a problem of its own, wouldn't it?

Our spiritual life looks about the same. We wake up and pray, "Grant, O Lord, to keep us this day without sin." The next words out of our mouth acknowledge the impossibility of that, as we implore, "O Lord have mercy upon us, have mercy upon us."[31] We sin. We confess our sin. We receive absolution. And we wake up the next day and do it all over again. The life of the baptized is not a constant, steady climb to perfection. It looks more like a circle, as we return to our Baptism daily.

So if you feel like you're chasing your tail, that's to be expected. You're alive! Period.

---

31 Te Deum, (*LSB*, p. 225, st. 9).

WHEN LIFE GIVES YOU LEMONADE

A tornado charges down the street, leaving one house a mangled mess while the neighbor's is virtually unscratched. People naturally wonder about the experience of the survivors who crawl out of the basement of the destroyed home. What about those who climb the basement stairs to find their house in perfect condition in the face of devastating damage just yards away?

This is life on the planet earth. Some are facing terrible tragedies of one kind or another and some just . . . aren't. Of course, no life is completely free from trouble—Christ in His Word has made this clear (John 16:33). There are times, though, when our troubles are really small by comparison.

There is the woman who walks out of the imaging center having found out that her lump was not cancer. There is the woman with a good boss and reliable, rewarding employment. There is the woman whose family is happy and blessed.

To cast the net even wider, there are people who are born in the twenty-first century in the United States of America. Yes, there are people who have clean running water, food in ample supply, and electricity twenty-four hours out of every day with only occasional exceptions for strong winds or ice storms. In fact, this probably applies to every person reading these words.

When you are blessed, you could feel embarrassed or unworthy or even guilty on account of how good you've got it. You might ask God why you were born to a life in a secure home with carpeting and insulated walls on a quiet street while others were born to a life in a dirt-floor shack with a corrugated tin roof. You could live with a sense of foreboding, thinking you must be due for trouble any day now. You could invent or imagine some problems in your life because having it so good feels unnatural and unsustainable.

We all understand that we're to trust in God and His provision and protection amid troubles, but sometimes in the absence of troubles, we aren't sure just what to do with ourselves. For all the rich blessings in our life, we feel terrible for those without. We know that though we walked out of the women's health center with a clear test result, there are many who didn't. While we enjoy our work, there are others without—and very much in need. Compared to our household's occasional disagreement or misunderstanding, there are some with chronic unhappiness. Our child contracts and recovers from a stomach bug while our cousin's child continues to wait and wait for a heart transplant.

Those who suffer often ask God "Why?" to try to understand their trials. When we see the suffering in the world around us, we may ask God that "why" question from another angle. Why do I live in such a state of prosperity? Why don't I face financial hardship? Why are my loved ones and I happy and healthy and well?

The Lord owes no answer to this question, regardless of who's asking it and for what reason. He does, however, have a few things to say that may or may not satisfy but are nevertheless His Word.

"Where were you when I laid the foundation of the earth? Tell Me, if you have understanding." (Job 38:4)

But who are you, O man, to answer back to God? Will what is molded say to its molder, "Why have you made me like this?" (Romans 9:20)

Your life is your life because the Lord ordained it for you. If your closets and pantry are full, it's because He's seen to it. If you are healthy, that's His doing too. If your family is happy and well, He is to thank. When you are blessed, rejoice and be glad. He made you that way. Rather than ask "Why?" first say "Thank You" to your heavenly Father, who has been so very good to you—far beyond what you deserve.

Next, ask "How?" and "Where?" How can you care for others whose lives are harder? Where can you serve using the gifts and resources that you have in abundance?

Romans 12:3–8 acknowledges that gifts of grace are not doled out uniformly. Our giving is no more than an extension of what we have first received. It is gauged proportionately. The one who is called to contribute should do so in generosity—having received much and therefore having much to give. The one who does acts of mercy is called to carry this out with cheerfulness.

Second Corinthians 8:14 gives more clear instruction: "Your abundance at the present time should supply their need."

Martin Chemnitz explained the "haves and have-nots" crisis years ago: "For God has distributed the human race into two categories: (1.) There are some who possess wealth, to whom the commandment has been delivered concerning the giving of alms. (2.) There are some needy people, who are to be helped by alms, as the Scripture says (Deuteronomy 15:11), 'There will not fail to be poor people in the land where you will dwell.' No third category, i.e., those who neither are in need nor give, can be found in the Scripture."[32]

God determines the distributions and, if you're in that first category, you are there according to His wisdom and will. It shouldn't embarrass or cause guilt. You're not a bad person for having been blessed as you have. When you feel that you have more than you need, you're right! You are *richly* blessed!

Fill up the offering plate because you can. Donate your hair or sew a scarf to provide warmth and covering for a woman whose hair is gone. Invite people to your home because you have one and it is warm, comfortable, and happy. Visit others in their affliction because you have the health and strength to walk to their room and to sit at their bedside while they are laid low. Offer a ride to the person who can't drive to church because her eyes are failing. Don't feel bad that you have it so good. Feel good that you can use all of those blessings in service to others whose lives aren't as easy as yours.

See the Lord at work behind everything that is going well for you. He has a plan for those blessings beyond your own comfort, and possibly beyond your own comfort zone. When life gives you lemonade, raise your glass high, give thanks, and share it. Cheers!

---

32 Martin Chemnitz, *On Almsgiving*, trans. James A. Kellerman (St. Louis: LCMS World Relief and Human Care, 2004), 11–12.

The Belle Choir: A Parochial Fantasy

Our Lady of the Reformation Lutheran Church has a women's music group that meets every Wednesday evening. Miss Angela Belle is the director. The other members of the group (in order of appearance) are: Prudence, Victoria, Concordia, Serena, Constance, Joy, Felicity, twins Pearl and Ruby, Dolores, Grace, Sophia, Gloria, Valerie, Faith, Charity, Harmony, Hope, and Dora.

Curtain opens.

A din of high-ish-pitched chatter fills the music room, and heels of varying lengths plunk clicks on the tile floor. Many perfumes occupy the same small space to create awkward wafting.

ANGELA: *(Clapping her hands together a few times)* Okay, ladies, let's all find our places. I know you have a lot to talk about, but it's time to get practicing. As you know, we will provide the preservice music this weekend and we have a lot to get through tonight.

PRUDENCE: *(Raising her hand sensibly)* I'm sorry to ask this, but do you think it's a good idea to continue with the plan to perform this weekend? As of last Wednesday evening, there were still a lot of issues to work through.

VICTORIA: *(Head high and with triumphant conviction)* Prudence, you're not nearly confident enough. This round of songs is going to be one of the best our church has ever heard!

(CONCORDIA *shifts in her chair and clears her throat in an attempt to put an end to the conversation. Disagreements of any sort tend to make her uncomfortable.*)

PRUDENCE: Well, Victoria, you seem to think winning is your birthright, but some of us have found through thoughtful observation and careful consideration that charging ahead isn't always what's right or best.

(SERENA *takes slow, deep breaths and docilely twirls a strand of silky hair. She's thinking about her upcoming weekend at the lake. She's going to miss the performance. She's totally fine with that. She calmly wonders if she's mentioned this to* ANGELA *. . . "Well, maybe another time," she thinks as she finds a new strand for twirling.*)

CONSTANCE: Prudence and Victoria both offer fine perspectives, but what's most important is that we follow the lead of our director. Miss Belle, you know what's best, and we're all behind you!

ANGELA: Thank you, Connie. I appreciate that. Yes, I think we will be ready. By now the bulletin has been printed. There are still a few areas that need work, but that is what we're here for tonight. Maybe some of you will be able to come back on Friday for a final rehearsal, just to be sure we've got it down.

JOY: Yes!!!! That sounds great! I'll definitely be there, and I can't wait!

FELICITY: I'm with Joy!

PEARL and RUBY: (Chiming in almost in unison) We can't make it because it's our little brother's birthday on Friday.

ANGELA: Don't worry about that, dears. You two are gems. We're just glad that you're in our group, even though you're busy with high school and family activities. We need more young people like you!

DOLORES: I don't know if I can come on Friday either. I'm here tonight and I hope to be here on Sunday, but my back pain has been worse than usual . . .

VICTORIA: Stiff upper lip, Dolores! You can do it!

GRACE: Let's go easy on Dolores.

VICTORIA: I wasn't being hard on her. I was cheering her on!

GRACE: Quite right. I was too hard on you, Victoria.

(SERENA gently traces the stitched lines of her music folder. She softly hums the line of the opening song to herself.)

SOPHIA: (Overhearing SERENA's hum) Maybe we should actually start rehearsing?

ANGELA: Yes. Yes, we should. Thank you, Sophia. A wise suggestion! From the top then, here we go . . .

(Two pages in, ANGELA waves them all to stop.)

ANGELA: This section here on page 4 is marked pianissimo, but I'm hearing quite a bit of volume coming from the back of the room.

GLORIA: *(Loudly!)* Sorry! That's my bad! It's hard to rein it in sometimes. I guess I'm more of a *forte* specialist! Ha-ha!

ANGELA: *(Reining it in on GLORIA's behalf)* That's alright, Gloria. We need that strength in other places. Maybe you could circle the "*pp*" on page 4 as a reminder to yourself.

GLORIA: *(Still loudly!)* I can do that! *(Circles the "pp" noisily)* Sorry to stop the show! Let's keep going and I'll take it down a notch!!!
(PEARL and RUBY look at each other and giggle. GLORIA is loud even when she's talking about being quiet.)

ANGELA: *(Raises her baton patiently and smiles prettily)* Very good. From the top of page 2 then, and this time we'll all watch the dynamics more closely.

(The group continues until the end of the first piece.)

ANGELA: That was pretty good! Let's take out the next one. There are a few bars that will sound better as a solo. Is anyone willing to take it?

VALERIE: *(Bravely)* I haven't done a solo before, but I would like to try.

ANGELA: What courage! How wonderful. Thank you!

FAITH: You'll do great, Valerie. I believe in you.

(VALERIE handles her solo, navigating a few tricky places without any indication that she's nervous or afraid.)
(The song continues. At one point, DOLORES sits down and gingerly rubs her lower back. The metal chair doesn't feel

much better than standing, but it's all she has. CHARITY leaves the room without a word.)

ANGELA: *(Directing the final bars of the song and waving her hand for a robust finish)* Excellent! That really sounded good, and the solo at the beginning was just what we needed.

FELICITY: I'm so happy you took that solo, Valerie.

JOY: So am I!

(CHARITY enters the room with a couch cushion under her arm. It must have come from the church library. Without a word, she hands the cushion to DOLORES and nods lovingly before returning to her place. DOLORES gives a pained smile of thanks.)

ANGELA: It's settled then. The solo is Valerie's, and we're glad she'll take it for us. Let's run through the third song now. This one is our hardest, so we'll need some extra time to work on it.

(The group begins to work through the third song with effort . . . and errors.)

ANGELA: Okay, let's take a break. The real problems begin at measure 28.

HARMONY: Could you play each part separately? We can't hear our own notes, and it's all coming out a mess.

ANGELA: That's a good idea. Let's take each part on its own and see if that helps.

(Plays each part several times until each group is more successful independently)

ANGELA: Good! Let's try to put it all together now!

HOPE: We've worked so hard. It's bound to be better.

(Cacophony, but of a slightly lesser degree)

JOY: I think it sounds better!

FELICITY: I think so too!

HARMONY: Ehhhh . . . at least we tried . . .

ANGELA: We can iron out those final wrinkles on Friday. It's getting late. Let's plan to practice again Friday at seven for those who are able.

CONSTANCE: We're all behind you, Miss Belle.

DORA: I will bring something for everyone who comes!

ANGELA: How sweet. Thank you, Dora. You're such a giving person. And thank you, everyone, for giving of yourselves in service to the Lord and His Church.

Curtain closes.

THANK YOU

Joyce and +Elsie

Jan, Karen, and Donita

Cheryl, Dawn, Katie, Abra, Lisa

Peggy, Elizabeth, and Lindsey

Dr. Scaer

Dan, Heath, Scott, and Jack

And Joel, for being the only person in the family who didn't do anything to help.